Between Worlds:
My Life As a Missionary Kid
By Simeon Harrar

Table of Contents:

D1516818

Preface

My name is Simeon Harrar. Growing up as a missionary kid (MK) meant that much of the time I felt like I dreamt up my childhood. I replay all the crazy stories about headhunters, jungles and jellyfish and wonder if somewhere along the way I conjured them up out of thin air because my real life was mundane. Most of my adult life I have walked around with an abundance of images and memories hidden away as if there were a stranger living inside of me. The stories have gone untold, buried beneath layers of fear and forgetfulness. In many ways my life has been incomplete, a half-life, a partial tale even to those who know me best.

When I came home to America as a scrawny 18-year-old college student I spent vast amounts of time trying to make sense of this new world. I learned the lingo, bought a new wardrobe and caught up on the past decade or two of pop culture via Yahoo, Blockbuster and Ask Jeeves (it was a thing back in the day). I applied myself full-time to fitting in, but the more I listened to the pulse of the culture, the more I realized there was another pulse beating simultaneously within me. It was the pulse of Papua New Guinea and Africa: the pulse of the distant lands of my childhood and all the people and places that had formed me.

Their collective voices sing, shout and whisper into my ears even today. I see their faces and their scars.

I feel their pain and their confusion. They are a part of me, burned into my memory and tattooed across my heart.

So just like the 18-year-old version of myself, I am still in this strange place—between worlds. I am a man without a home, yet with a hundred doors always open wide to me. I am a sojourner, both addicted to the road and tired of always being on the move. I have an American passport, but this is not my true home. I speak several languages, but I'm often at a loss for words in all of them. It is a palpable tension being from two worlds at once. It is both a blessing and a curse.

As you read this book, I hope you will laugh and cry at my family's humorous attempts to find a synthesis of these different cultures. Somewhere along the way, I hope you will come to understand what it was like growing up between worlds.

Chapter 1
Life as I Knew It

Missionaries are always on the move between worlds. It comes with the territory. You spend a few years overseas and then there's a long journey back home for a year, which is just long enough to get acclimated before you are whisked overseas again. After a while, all the packing and planes become part of the rhythm of doing life.

Boxes and Bakers

Let me give you a brief rundown of my family's moving history. (If this were a commercial, the next few paragraphs would be read at rapid speed!) My parents met at a conference in Dallas, Texas. They courted and got engaged over HAM radio while working in different South American countries. Talk about romantic...umm... not exactly.

When it became unsafe where they were working, they took on a new assignment in Papua New Guinea. Not a big deal. Just hop on a plane and fly to the middle of the Pacific Ocean on the other side of the world. It was there my sister and I were born. I was about a year old when my family returned briefly to America and then moved to Quebec, Canada. From the Tropics to the arctic cap, we were quickly covering the entire globe. Braving the extreme cold for two years, my parents attended French language school, and we kids saw more snow than we would for the next 18 years combined.

Somewhere in there my brother was born, weighing in at over ten pounds, much to the amazement of all the petite Canadian women and much to the relief of my poor mother, who had slowly grown to the size of a tugboat. Once language training was complete our family of five headed back to the Equator. Senegal, Africa was calling our name, and a whole new world of sun and sand awaited us.

We lived right along the beach in Dakar. A city transformed from the quiet days of French Colonialism to a sprawling, growing, overcrowded city on the edge of the desert. We were just one more family joining the crowd.

I toddled along in the hot sand, holding my mother's hand in the bright morning sunlight. My thin bleach-blonde hair danced around my head as the cool ocean breeze bid us good morning. Like most other mornings, we were on our way to the little bakery around the corner. My miniature blue flip-flops struggled in the thick sand, but I trudged forth with great determination. Awaiting me was a fresh French baguette.

Our final destination was not like your average American bakery. If you are imagining a cute brick building with an inviting bakery sign hanging over a large glass window displaying an array of fresh breads and pastries calling invitingly to those passing by, then you couldn't be more wrong.

I released my mom's hand and ran across the last stretch of scorching sand to the unfinished cinder block building where, in my four-year-old opinion, God himself baked bread every day just for me. The enterprise gave credence to the phrase "a hole in the wall." I slapped the necessary coinage down on the bread counter and greeted the baker. He picked up the coins, feeling them between his fingers, and then from underneath the counter pulled a baguette wrapped gently in yesterday's newspaper. The bread was warm to the touch and left my hands lightly powdered with white flower. It took all my self-control not to tear the long loaf in two so I could dig out the soft, fluffy inside.

My attention went back to the baker. I stared at him and he stared back unblinking. His milky eyes gazed past me toward the white-capped ocean, although he could no longer see the waves. He swam in an unending ocean of black as he filled the world with baguettes fit for a king. Before losing his sight to cataracts, he was a judo master and personal bodyguard for the president of Senegal. Hands forever dusted with flour standing out against his midnight skin, he taught judo once a week to the young men in the community. People came from all over to learn self-defense from the blind baker.

Dressed in my little white judo outfit with my white belt proudly on display, I joined the ranks of boys in a circle in the baker's sweltering little training room to learn the art of self-defense. We sat on thin mats that smelled of generations of sweaty boys. As usual, I was paired up against my chunky African neighbor. He was about my size but had an enormous bald head. We were quite the spectacle wrapped up in our heavy white judo robes trying to look tough. The Baker made his way to the center of the circle and demonstrated a sequence of new moves. They all looked the same to me.

After the instruction was over my neighbor and I made our way to the middle of the circle while everyone watched. Huffing and puffing, we attempted to trip and throw each other like we'd just seen, but it looked more like some strange, frantic dance that ended with us sprawled on the mat. Like the fish in the marketplace just a few hundred yards away, we flopped about gasping for breath until neither of us could go on. The match was called. There was no winner, and neither of us would be progressing past white belts anytime soon.

After all the matches, the Baker would let the older boys try to throw him down and put him on his back. One after the other they ended up laying on the matt staring up into the face of the the Baker. He was as immovable as a mountain. His powerful hands gripped his opponent and refused to let go. His stocky legs were rooted on the mat. Not once did the blind tree fall. Not once did his sweat mingle with ours on the mats. I stared at his cloudy, wandering eyes as the wind whipped outside and the sun beat down. I felt the sweat pool under my eyes and I tugged at my double-knotted belt. The blind black belt Baker was the first person to break into my safe little world and force me to see things I had never known were possible. He would not be the last.

The Old Headhunter

I was born in a miniature clinic with drab wooden walls and a corrugated iron roof high in the tropical mountains of Papua New Guinea. There was no asking for an epidural, no emergency room if things went badly, just a lot of hot water, prayers and my mother's painful perseverance through 18 long hours of labor. The nearest state of the art hospital was an entire country away. There was no crowd of anxious family members milling about in the waiting room, no balloons, or teddy bears or cell phones waiting to capture the first beautiful moments of life.

Half a world away, soon-to-be grandmothers, aunts and uncles carried on with their daily lives, oblivious to my wailing arrival. Only later through the garbled static of a long-distance phone call (which cost about as much as my total medical bill) was the good news shared. Little baby Simeon was safe and sound. It took another couple of months for the first pictures of me dressed up in second-hand clothes with my chubby cheeks on full display to make their way across numerous oceans and into the waiting hands of gray-haired grandparents.

I was conceived, carried and brought into the world on this beautiful island. I took my first breaths of crisp air amid its high mountains and lush jungles, alongside its wild, twisting rivers. My parents were young American missionaries with Wycliffe Bible

Translators, so my passport said I was American. But the seal of the stars and stripes did not tell the whole story. There was another flag with a cluster of stars and a Bird of Paradise against a red and black background flying over my life. I was a child of two worlds, and Papua New Guinea was my first.

I was born into this exotic world in 1987. Papua New Guinea was and is one of the last uncharted frontiers on Earth, a mystical world of jungles and swamps and mist-covered mountains surrounded by magnificent oceans. Mostly unpopulated, this tropical island supports pockets of people who live off the land as hunters and farmers, carving out their existence on the sides of steep mountains just like their ancestors did for centuries before them. Tied to the alternating seasons of rain and dry for survival, they lived largely untouched by the trappings of Western expansion.

I was just a white, squealing newborn when my parents brought me out to the neighboring village to visit our national friends. Most of the villagers had never seen a white baby, so they came to take a look at this unusual sight. Passed around from one set of curious arms to the next the gazing villagers laughed and "tsked" at my pale skin and constant squirming. There is something universally inviting about children that transcends even the most expansive cultural barriers and draws people together.

After the game of hot potato ran its course, I ended up with one of the village's old men. Lean and wiry, the warrior and hunter, held himself with a dangerous confidence. Nestled awkwardly in his dark powerful arms, which were much more comfortable shooting arrows and throwing spears than holding tiny babies, I looked up into his ebony face, unsure of what to make of this stranger. In days gone by he was a headhunter well versed in the art of battle. Beneath his short graying hair and observant brown eyes hung a large bone pierced through his thick nose.

My older sister, Dreya, waddled over to our unusual pairing, wondering who this fearsome man was holding her, "little baby Cinnamon." It was years before she could pronounce my name correctly. Dreya watched as my wandering chubby hands reached up greedily at the strange object protruding from the man's nose. Being a good sister she took matters into her own hands.

Without hesitation, my sister's pale, plump fingers reached out and gripped the polished bone piercing. Somewhere in the background rose my father's elongated "Noooooooooo..." as he saw what was about to take place. He was too late.

The old warrior's face contorted in pain as the bone was quickly jerked right out of his nostrils. Delivering her gift to me, my sister smiled with glee as I received my newfound treasure by shaking it like a rattle. The old man with his tribal tattoos and chorded muscles slowly turned toward my shocked parents, making eye contact with them as they cringed in disbelief at what had just happened.

A sly grin crept across his face. Laughing out loud, he rescued his nose bone from my tight-fisted grasp. My sister scampered off, and my parents dared to breathe again. As for me, I kept right on gurgling, completely unaware of the near crisis. Welcome to the unexpected world of a missionary kid!

Batman

Every country has its own set of superheroes. During my time in Sengal, Africa I fell in love with their tall tales and watched their TV shows, even though I wasn't supposed to. But at the end of the day it was an American superhero who won my heart: Batman.

My sister, Dreya, is a year and nine months older than me. As a child I thought she was just a few rungs below Batman on the "cool" ladder. I followed her around and did whatever she told me to do, and believe me when I tell you she was more than happy to boss me around.

I stood before Dreya beaming under my black plastic mask and makeshift cape, momentarily pausing my patrol around the house as the protector of Gotham. Underneath my costume I was proudly wearing nothing but my multicolored Batman undies. Saving Gotham was sweaty work in the nearly 100-degree Senegalese temperatures. Shirts and shorts were optional for my current mission, and a popsicle would have been greatly appreciated to honor my many deeds of heroism on behalf of the Barbies and stuffed animals scattered around the house.

Playing off my childhood superhero crush, my sister advised me that there was an opening for a new Batman. My ears perked up. I already had the cape and the mask, so I was halfway there. "Simeon," she said sternly, "you need to begin training immediately if you want to have any chance at becoming the next Batman." I nodded my head vigorously. Much to my surprise, Dreya volunteered to be my training coach. I swirled my cape with excitement. This was just getting better and better. Though lacking a whistle, clipboard and any other necessary superhero training credentials, Dreya proceeded to sneak us out of the house and up to the top of an unfinished two-story building a couple of houses down from ours for our first workout. Once there, she explained to me my task. To begin my training and prove my bravery, I would have to jump off the roof. Apparently she was taking a "go big or go home" approach to her new coaching role.

I stood on top of the partially completed building, clinging to the steel tie rods protruding from the roof, and stared down at the sand far below. It was riddled with discarded cement bricks and broken glass. There was a stiff, salty sea breeze blowing and somewhere in the background stood my sister with her freckled nose and blonde hair, an unlikely villain if ever there was one. Everything swam before my eyes, and I squinted, feeling seasick, as if I were on the crow's nest of a massive ship. Unsure what technique to use, I did the only thing I knew how to do. I leapt off the roof and felt my body suspended in the air weightless as the wind held me up, and then my arch nemesis, gravity, kicked in, and I tucked into a cannon ball and headed straight for my doom.

I don't remember hitting the ground. All I recall is getting to my little feet with my legs all covered in sand, and somewhere far above, the horrified face of my sister hovered as the gravity (pun possibly intended) of what she'd just asked me to do sank in.

Miraculously I managed to avoid the cinder blocks and broken glass and did not so much as roll my ankle—I walked away completely unharmed! My sister immediately put further Batman training on hold. Running around in my Batman undies and black cape would have to suffice for a while. She then made me swear we would not tell my parents at all about "The Jump" until I turned 13, at which point my training could continue. This silence was the next stage of my preparation, she said. So for the love of Batman, I held my tongue.

Little did I realize that my sister's superhero training course was preparing me for my "real" life as a missionary kid. When I returned to the United States on furlough I often felt like a superhero walking around trying to act normal while underneath the false front I had an amazing secret identity. People looked at me without a clue that I had a whole life and world of experiences they could barely imagine. I didn't reveal my secret identity for fear of being mocked or misunderstood. People could not be trusted or they just didn't seem to care. Either way, I learned to to hold my tongue.

The Pig Bucket

My parents were really big on us doing chores growing up. We had to earn our keep. In fact, my father at one point tried to make us pay rent to live under his roof. Thankfully my mother told him he was out of his mind and advised him to drop the idea, but they were a united and determined front when it came to teaching us the value of hard work. As a result, I became well acquainted with the pig bucket. To this day I'm not entirely sure why we called it the pig bucket, but as far back as I can remember that's what we called it—even though we never had pigs. The pig bucket was the nasty receptacle in the kitchen where all of the food leftovers were tossed. Growing up on a tropical island (I'm not trying to rub this little fact in, I promise), we ate a lot of fresh fruits and vegetables. In fact, I think there were times when Mom would throw a few chicken scraps into the mix just to remind us what meat tasted like.

All of this fresh produce meant lots and lots of peelings and shavings made their way into the dreaded pig bucket where they would sit and ferment, so when you opened the lid you would get socked by a hot burst of rotting odor while you were "kamikazeed" by swarms of fruit flies.

Because I was the oldest boy and the "strongest," it was my job to empty the pig bucket when it was full. This was rather humorous because I was a puny little thing with the spindliest arms you ever saw, and by the time the bucket was full it probably weighed about as much as I did. So there I would go, heaving this nasty bucket while fermenting fruit remnants slopped all down my legs. Early on I had to take the bucket only a short distance, but then my parents learned about a new invention called composting, and I had to cart that awful bucket all the way down to the bottom of the yard and dump it in the banana patch.

But that was only half the battle. After emptying the bucket I had to rinse it out. We had an outside faucet with only one setting—full blast! You could hear the water rushing through the pipes picking up momentum before bursting out like a super soaker on steroids. So there I would be, holding the bucket at arm's length as water splashed and ricocheted off of it, spraying every which way. The last sticky food remnants flew at me and latched on like leaches. By the time it was all over I'd swallowed half a dozen fruit flies and needed a shower.

In 5th grade our family returned to the United States and I heard my classmates complaining about how their "terrible" parents forced them to make their beds and do other chores around the house. I tried to tell them about the dreaded pig bucket and they all looked at me like I was from another planet. "Why don't you just put the food in the garbage disposal and buy fertilizer for your plants? That's what we do."

Now it was my turn to look at them like they were from a different planet. "What's a garbage disposal?"

They all laughed at me as if I was some sort of idiot for not knowing what a garbage disposal was. I was an intruder in their world, but they didn't have to worry because I would be gone soon enough.

The Wheels on the Bus Go Round and Round

Papua New Guinea didn't have four seasons like in America. No golden leaves or winter wonderlands. Instead, we had dry season and rainy season. During the dry season you choked on dust, and in the rainy season the roads became a nearly impassible muddy mess. Cars squealed and sputtered and spun their wheels trying not to get stuck in the thick mud. They dragged themselves through small ponds, and when things were really bad, through rushing rivers of water running across the roads. It was on such a day, when the rains had been coming down something fierce for a couple of days straight and the roads had been churned up to look like a thick, red stew, that I piled onto the blue and white school bus to take the 15-minute ride to elementary school.

Right from the get-go the old bus struggled to get traction. We drove over the bridge leading out of the compound and the waters rushing by underneath us nearly overflowed their banks. This was the only road to school, so no matter what, there was no turning back. The bus slipped and lurched, weaving back and forth across the road trying to find the best path. All of us kids watched excitedly out the window as the bus splashed through enormous pothole after enormous pothole, sending up waves of water in its wake. We came around the bend and were nearly at school when the bus met its match.

With half the road eroded into what looked like a small swimming pool, the bus came to a wheel-screeching halt. The bus driver instructed all of us kids to pile into the back to give the vehicle more weight and create traction, but our skinny little missionary kid bodies didn't do much good: the bus was good and stuck. We all poured out of the bus like ants and waded barefoot into the mud to help push the bus free. We grunted and groaned, pushing with all our might as the bus's spinning wheels sprayed mud everywhere. By the time the bus was free we were covered in mud and looked like we'd been shot by a bunch of red paintballs. Those of us who were really dirty like me had to walk the rest of the way to school.

We were all late and strolled proudly into our classrooms with mud-red hand-me-downs and splatter marks on full display. The teachers rolled their eyes and directed us to the back row of seats. We opened up our backpacks and pulled out science textbooks and pencils as if nothing out of the ordinary had happened. There would be no phone calls home for fresh clothes as the muddy clay dried red and flaky peeling off like sunburned skin. This was just another day in the life of a missionary kid.

A Very Special Class

In middle school all the guys in my grade—about twelve to fifteen of us depending on who was home on furlough—had one elective class together each semester. We took Home Economics, during which I managed to nearly burn down the whole building when I forgot to turn the oven off one day after class. After I spent weeks working to sew a pair of boxers, they completely fell apart the first time through the wash.

Next, we moved on and had a class on puppetry. Who knew puppeteers were such artists? What I really learned was just how much pain I could endure while trying to hold my arms up over my head for the duration of a five-minute song. We spent almost the whole semester working on a performance based on the song "Shut the door, keep out the devil." We played that crazy song over and over again until I heard it in my sleep. Maybe if we'd been a little bit more focused we wouldn't have spent basically an entire semester on one song, but what can you expect from a bunch of middle school boys with puppets?

After the puppets it became clear that our teachers were running out of options for us, so they had a mother from the community come in and teach us how to make a quilt. Sewing boxers was bad enough. By the time I was done butchering my quilt with crooked lines and lumpy batting, I was about ready to take a baseball bat to the ancient Singer sewing machine I'd been assigned. I gave the quilt to my mother as a gift and, like my boxers, the first time through the wash the darn thing fell to pieces. So much for my sewing career.

Now if puppetry and quilting weren't strange enough, our final middle school elective was a course on PNG survival skills. They really had to dig deep for this one, but man, it was the most awesome class ever! We spent the entire semester learning how to start fires without matches, set traps and do all sorts of other exciting things. For a bunch of middle school missionary boys it was like a dream come true. To cap off the semester, we all traveled out to the instructor's village for a field trip where we spent the weekend hiking and hanging out with the villagers.

While we were there, one of the old men in the village eagerly brought a couple of us into his round grass hut to show us something. Once our eyes adjusted to the darkness, I could make out a large pile of 50-kilogram bags stacked against the back wall. Grinning ear to ear, he proudly pointed to them and started telling us excitedly in Pidgin (the local trade language) that all of this was dried marijuana from his garden, which he then proceeded to show us. We were all very impressed in a mischievous sort of way.

Then, as any generous host would do, he offered us

some of his stash. Being good Christian missionary kids, we didn't want to be rude, so...we asked ourselves the logical question: "What would Jesus do?" Unfortunately there's no real protocol in the Gospels about what to do when offered marijuana by a stranger, and there hadn't been anything in our PNG survival skills class about this issue either.

Our host must have sensed our indecision and assured us the marijuana was of the highest quality. Yep, that was it, he surmised—we were worried about the quality of his organic weed! Finally, we decided if our parents ever found out we had tried some, the excuse that we did so only to be polite wasn't going to hold much weight. Most of us would be grounded until the rapture. While still agreeing it was a tempting offer, we chose to pass. But the old man just solidified our opinion—PNG Survival Skills was the best class ever!

Welcome to America?

My family came back to the US for furlough when I was in 10th grade. My parents enrolled my sister and me at a large public high school in Maryland. We were going from a school with about 200 students from 7th through 12th grade to a school with about 2500 students from 9th through 12th—just a slight difference between the two!

My experience the first day of classes can only be compared to walking through a crowded airport. The halls filled up with students jostling as they funneled through the long corridors trying to hurry to their next class as quickly as possible. In Papua New Guinea we had about 20 classrooms total, and we walked outside to change from one room to the next. There was no need for crowd control or cops. In Maryland, I felt like I was being swallowed up by an enormous mass of nameless faces. In PNG I knew everybody and everybody knew me. Here I knew nobody and nobody knew me. I became just another vanilla face in the crowd. I held on to the straps of my backpack for dear life and prayed I would be able to find my next classroom.

To my delight, my aunt worked at the high school as the Librarian. She graciously showed my sister and me around the buildings before school started to help us become acclimated. With our class schedules in hand she tried to make sure we knew where we were going. Unfortunately, it was a failed effort. The problem was that the building was so big, and every room and hallway looked the same. On the first day of classes I still managed to get miserably lost. Two of my classes were at opposite ends of the school, and I had to half power walk, half jog to get from one to the next on time. The first day I didn't make it, and as I walked into the classroom late everybody stared at me. I wondered if they could all tell I was a new kid with no idea what I was doing. I was so embarrassed.

It took me a couple of weeks before I managed to find my locker, so I carried all of my books around in my bag the whole day. When I finally found it, it was so far out of the way of all my classes that I never had time to go and use it. So I lumbered through the halls weighed down by about 20 pounds of books most days. I missed PNG.

During my first week of class I raised my hand and asked to go to the bathroom. I had been holding it for quite some time, hoping to be able to wait until the period was over, but my bladder wasn't cooperating. When the teacher acknowledged my request, I jumped up and darted out of the door. In PNG there was only one bathroom. Here in this building on this floor, I had no idea where the bathroom was. Afraid that at any moment I might explode, I was practically running through the halls trying to find the toilet, but to no avail. As I turned a corner I finally saw the little sign I'd been looking for.

Freedom was at my fingertips. Suddenly I heard a voice calling out, "Hey you! Stop!"

I didn't wait. I couldn't hold it. I made a beeline for the bathroom to relieve myself. When I stepped out into the hall there was a stern-looking adult staring at me asking, "Where's your hall pass?"

I looked at him inquisitively. "What's a hall pass?"

"Don't play games with me. If you don't have a hall pass, then you're going to the office."

"I'm sorry; I didn't know I needed to have a hall pass." I was getting nervous. I hadn't done anything wrong, I just needed to go the bathroom; that was it, and now I was going to be escorted down to the principal's office. What if they suspended me? This was crazy.

"You know the rules. Let's go!"

Just then one of my classmates, Adam, came around the corner waving his arms. "Wait!" he shouted. When he reached us he was breathing almost too heavily to blurt out, "I have two hall passes. One is for him."

He pointed at me.

The hall monitor glared in my direction. "Okay, but don't let it happen again." Then he walked away.

I wanted to explain to him that I grew up on an island

in the South Pacific where you didn't need a hall pass to use the bathroom. You just go. I wasn't a bad student up to no good. I wasn't smoking in the bathroom stalls or selling drugs. I just didn't know the rules. I wasn't like everybody else around here who seemed to know exactly what was going on. I didn't grow up here. I was a foreigner, but my American accent and Caucasian skin would have made those claims just sound like more lies. This is the problem with being a missionary kid: on the surface you blend in, but underneath you really have no idea what's going on.

Lunch was possibly the worst 30 minutes of the day. In PNG I had a whole hour and walked home for lunch and ate with my family. There was no cafeteria. No terrible plastic-tasting food. No awkward sitting with strangers. No fights needing to be broken up.

On my first day I found an empty seat at the end of a table and quietly ate my bag lunch without making eye contact with anyone. For the first few weeks I floated around to different tables wherever I could find a seat. Finally I landed at one of the nerdy loser tables where a couple of the kids I'd met in my English class sat. There I remained as one more strange member on the island of misfit boys. The conversations around the lunch table provided some of the most appalling and fascinating moments of culture shock for me. I was opened to a whole new world of vocabulary and topics. It was a crash course in pop culture, sex education and post-modern religious beliefs. These were not quite the same conversations that took place around our family table at home in PNG. It was there, in a US high school, around a plastic table, in 30-minute spurts, that I really became Americanized.

Equipment Failure

While living in Maryland I decided to try out for the high school basketball team. I had no idea the type of culture shock I was in for. I walked into the gym and stared in awe for a moment at the hard wood court. I'd never actually played on a real wooden court. I felt like I was walking into one of the great basketball arenas I'd been imagining since I was a little kid shooting hoops in my backyard.

I could hardly believe it when there were already about 100 guys milling about waiting for try-outs to start. Everyone was wearing brand new gear, well almost everyone. I was just wearing my regular sneakers and tennis shorts. Apparently I missed the dress code announcement. I shrank to the back of the crowds and waited to see what would happen next.

The coach walked to the middle of the court and blew his whistle. There was immediate silence. From that moment on I felt like I was in *Remember the Titans* with Denzel Washington. For the next two and a half hours we did nothing but run. Lap after lap and then seemingly endless suicides. It was insanity. People were puking into garbage cans and hiding in the bathroom. Americans were crazy!

This was a far cry from our laid back practices in PNG where we pretty much just did layup drills and scrimmaged against each other. There were parents sitting in the stands watching their kids. It was day one of practice and they were already hovering. By the end of the first week most of the guys had quit or been cut, including me. Apparently I wasn't cut out for this type of competition.

Later in the season I decided to go watch a game. My grandfather dropped me off at the gym and handed me $5. "You'll need this to get into the game." I took the money and stared at it. I couldn't believe you had to pay to see a high school game, but when I get into the gym I understood. There was not an empty seat in the house and the place was jumping. Apparently we were playing our cross-town rivals. The home team ran out onto the court and everyone went crazy. The players had slick matching uniforms and were all business. From the first tip-off it was a mad house. I'd never been to a sporting event with so much energy. Before I knew it I was on my feet yelling and screaming with everyone else. One of our guys hit a shot at the buzzer to win the game and I thought people were going to storm the court. It was absolute pandemonium.

I could still feel my adrenaline pumping on the way home from the the game. I'd played basketball my whole life, but what I'd just witnessed was like an entirely different sport.

In PNG our season consisted of two meagre tournaments against schools from the surrounding areas. You never even knew who was going to show up or when. PNG time is a little more fluid than American time, but getting folks to show up was only half the fun.

The PNG people as a whole are subsistence farmers who live off the land. Their high schools could barely afford to pay their teachers, let alone have a thriving athletic department. This became very apparent when their starting five stepped out onto the court.

They rarely had matching jerseys, and you would see players in all manner of shorts and even jeans. Then there were the shoes. Most of the teams would show up barefoot to play on our outdoor cement court. According to international rules, all players had to wear some type of footwear to play, so during substitutions the guy going to the bench would step out of his flip-flops and the guy coming in for him would slip them on. The fact that they were playing in flip-flops was humorous enough, but then you'd see one of them in a pair two or three sizes too big trying to run down the court and you'd hear the oversized flip-flops slapping the pavement with every step. These were cheap flip-flops, and next thing you know the strap would break, and in the middle of the play the guy would take the flip-flop off and start fixing it. The whole thing was just too much.

As I lay down to sleep I could still hear the cheering in my head and see the beautiful court and the perfect matching uniforms. America was a different world. One that I longed to be a part of but feared I would never understand.

Look Out for Jellyfish

Whenever our family came back to the States, we kids begged and pleaded with our parents to take us to Chuck E. Cheese. Going back to Chuck E. Cheese as an adult makes the place seem like it's losing its luster, but back then it was our version of heaven on earth—pizza, games and prizes galore. What could be better? For us Chuck E. Cheese was a symbol of all the fun things we weren't privileged to have because we lived overseas. As we grew older, malls and movie theaters became the more updated expressions of all that we were missing out on as we walked around in our out-of-date clothes. We either bought bootlegged copies of the most recent movies or waited months for them to come out on video so they could be shipped to us. No matter what, we were always behind or left to make do with a sub-par version of what consumeristic America was peddling, but from time to time living overseas had its advantages.

I stood holding my dad's hand looking down the long, gentle curve of the beach. I could see all the way to the giant domed mosque barely visible in the hazy distance. The whole way down, the sand was littered with bulbous, bubblegum-pink jellyfish. Twice a year during low tide thousands of these odd-looking creatures would become stranded on the beach and lay there looking like oversized Bazooka gum bubbles with tentacles. Together, Dad and I walked down to the sand, weaving in and out of the beached blobs and their stinging tentacles in nothing but our bare feet. Brandishing pointy driftwood sticks, we popped the beach invaders as fast as we could. It was the African version of the crazy Whac-A-Mole game you play at Chuck E. Cheese. There was no time limit though, no crowds of rowdy kids jostling for position with greasy mouths covered with pizza sauce, and no tokens to play. We laughed and ran and popped to our hearts' content.

New Shoes

In PNG you could always tell the MK's who had just returned from furlough because their shoes and clothes were still clean. It didn't last long, but for a few glorious days they reminded us of what the outside world was like. My sister's good friend Heidi was still giving off the furlough glow when she joined our family on a long hike. Sporting her brand new shoes from America that practically sparkled in the sunlight, making the rest of our footwear looked like decrepit at best. Our destination was a beautiful waterfall, but to get there we had to hike over miles of hot baking river rocks and wade through what seemed like a thousand streams, and beyond those obstacles the jungle awaited.

We'd barely begun when at the sight of the first stream Heidi decided she didn't want to ruin her shoes, so she promptly took them off. Wearing only her socks, she took on the smoldering river rocks. It was not really a fair fight considering that Heidi had been in the U.S. for a year and her feet had grown soft with the creature comforts of North American life. The thick calluses from years of walking around barefoot were gone, and pretty soon the hot sharp rocks began to take their toll. Heidi found a makeshift walking stick to ease the pain and kept singing at the top of her lungs to distract herself from the discomfort, but all her efforts were to no avail. My sister, Dreya, and Heidi tagged along in the rear, while Heidi moaned and groaned between verses. All she had to do was put on those fancy new sneakers and she would have been fine, but she refused. In a world of dirty sneakers and cheap flip flops there was something sacred about a pair of clean shoes.

We slowly reeled in the jungle that had once loomed far in the distance. Following a small dirt path, we pushed into the jungle, escaping the hot sun under the cover of the towering vine-covered trees. Our friend and trail guide, Wild Bill, vanished into the jungle for a second and reappeared with a large yellow pod cupped in his leathery hands and broke it in half for us to see. The inside was covered with white, slimy seeds that reminded me of slugs. "Try one," he advised.

Unsure what to expect, I gingerly placed a single seed in my mouth. I was immediately mesmerized with a deliciously sweet flavor so rich it made my tongue tingle with delight. I chewed and sucked on the seed until all the white coating was gone and spit the dark marble-sized seed into my hand, running my fingers over its smooth, shiny surface. It looked like something beautiful enough to be found on a fancy woman's necklace or a stone at the bottom of a glacier lake, but certainly not here.

Wild Bill smiled. "Any guesses what they use those seeds for?" he asked us.

I didn't have a clue as I stared blankly at him.

"Chocolate!" he informed us. "That right there is a cocoa seed. You'd have a lot of really unhappy people if those didn't exist."

When our nature lesson for the day was over, we kept walking along, mindlessly slurping on seeds and chatting away. Poor Heidi was now suffering badly as she encountered the roots and sticks and the occasional jagged stone. From time to time my brother and I would spot a cocoa tree and shimmy up the trunk to snag another cocoa pod or two. The really ripe ones were a warm orange color, and when we cracked them open we'd stuff as many seeds into our mouths as we possibly could until our cheeks were bulging, counting them to see who could hold the most—sort of like the old game, Chubby Bunnies. Then we'd walk along just sucking on them, letting the delicious juices mix with our saliva, leaving a string of sweet nectar running all the way down our throats to our bellies. What a marvelous mood God must have been in when he invented the cocoa pod!

At last we arrived at our destination. Nestled into the folded layers of pumice-like volcanic rock was an amazing fresh waterfall spilling about ten feet into a deep, clear pool. Up above there was a natural waterslide that fed into a second perfectly round but smaller pool. It was a magical place. Heidi rushed to the cold water to cool her blistering feet as her shoes sat safely away from the water on a large stone.

When it was time to go I was sure Heidi would succumb to the cries of her throbbing feet and put on her shoes. I was wrong. With her once white socks now turned the color of rich chocolate pulled up to her calves, Heidi leaned on her walking stick and led us home, singing all the way with her clean white shoes dangling over her shoulder.

An Epic Shot

In Papua New Guinea, my family lived on a missionary base called Ukarumpa. In many ways it was like a small rural American town. There was one post office, one school and one store. The nearest "town" was a good 30 minutes away. There were about 1200 of us from all over the world living together in our tiny community.

In the mornings Papua New Guinean men often set up shop just outside the store selling beautiful wooden carvings and bowls. I had little interest in these artsy things, but what grabbed my attention were the fully functioning bows and arrows for sale. My brother and I begged Dad to buy us a bow and some arrows, and of course he couldn't resist us. We came home with two bows, one very flexible little model made of bamboo and a second bow made of Limboom, a much stronger dark-colored wood. The bow was about as tall as I was.

The first thing we had to do was string the bows. The little bamboo bow was simple enough for both my brother and me, but neither of us could so much as budge the big bow. Even after Dad strung it for us, we couldn't pull back the string to get a shot off. Begrudgingly, we decided to take turns with the little one.

Next, Landon and I set up a small cardboard box on

one end of the yard and started our target practice. The arrows were slender bamboo shafts with long wooden heads tied together with a thick grass; they had no feathers. I was up first. Standing about 30 feet from the box, I took my aim, carefully pulling back the string as far as I could, and let it fly. I watched in amazement as the arrow arched far over our target and landed in the neighbor's yard. Oops! For some reason I had a feeling Mr. Bennett wasn't going to be terribly excited about us shooting arrows close to his house. I put down the bow and ran to retrieve my errant shot.

Meanwhile, Landon was getting impatient for his turn. The temptation was just too great. I was on my way back when I saw him pick up the bow and notch an arrow of his own. I was only a couple of feet behind the box and didn't think he'd actually shoot. Oh how wrong I was! He fired, and before I could move, the arrow flashed across the yard and buried itself in my foot. I stared in disbelief at the bamboo shaft protruding from between my toes and the blood trickling onto the thick bladed grass.

Enraged, I glared at Landon across the yard. His face had gone ghostly white. I felt a mad rush of adrenaline and anger coursing through my body along with the first wave of pain. If I could have put my hands on him I would have shook him like a rag doll. Landon knew it too, and made a mad dash for the house screaming "Mom!" at the top of his lungs. I pulled the arrow out of my foot and raced after him leaving a trail of blood across the yard. He slammed the door just before I could grab him. Inside he was safe, but he'd have to come out some time. I would be waiting.

The adrenaline was wearing off, and I began to feel my foot pulsing as the blood continued to run red. My revenge would have to be put on hold. I washed the puncture wound off with brown river water from the outside spigot before making my way to the bathroom. I pulled our bottle of hydrogen peroxide out from behind the mirror and poured it on my foot. I screamed in agony. The liquid burned like fire, frothing and bubbling as it cleaned out the injury. I was squeezing towel rack with all my might to keep from screaming when Mom came into the bathroom and found me with a fountain of bubbling hydrogen peroxide coming out of the hole in my foot. My brother was clinging to her dress in tears scared for his life, and it wasn't long before the whole story came out.

It almost goes without saying that we were grounded and forbidden to use the bow and arrows for a very long time. After a few weeks of punishment, during which the bow and arrows cruelly sat out in plain view but remained off limits, Dad gave us a strict lecture on bow safety and allowed us to resume our archery endeavors. But to this day Landon still owes me one for that epic shot.

Gumis

Growing up in Papua New Guinea there were no malls, movie theaters or TV stations. We had dial-up internet access with one server for the entire country, which meant even trying to check your email could take a half hour, depending on the day. Without all the typical American options to entertain ourselves, we had to come up with our own fun. This was not a problem for us.

Over the years my father had managed to acquire a number of rubber inner tubes pulled from old tractor and truck tires. We called them gumis. We would use them like rafts to float down the river on a lazy Saturday afternoon, but most of the time they sat underneath our house gathering dust. One day while rummaging around under the house, my brother and I had a brilliant idea. Our back yard had a nice big hill extending all the way down from our house to the road. The yard was filled with trees and bushes, and at a certain point there was a drop-off that had felled many an unsuspecting victim playing "capture the flag" in the dark. We decided to try and scrunch ourselves inside the gumis and roll down the hill as fast as we could, in spite of its obstacles. Think of it as the tropical equivalent to sledding, but with a much greater dizzying effect.

Next thing I knew, I was sitting at the top of the hill by the house. My head was tucked into the gumi, so I couldn't see what was in front of me. I rocked back to gain momentum and launched myself forward, pushing off with my feet as hard as I could. With each rotation I kicked off again, gaining more and more speed as I zipped between a large bush and the guava tree before veering slightly to the left, heading straight for the road. By this time I was moving so fast that everything was a blur and my head was spinning so much that I didn't really know where I was. In a moment of panic, I bailed out of the gumi. With arms and legs flailing, I eventually rolled to a stop, now covered in dirt and grass stains. I was so dizzy I could barely stand up, and I staggered around for a couple of steps before I lay back down on the grass and succumbed to a spinning world. At the top of the hill my brother was staring down with wide eyes and started yelling, "That was awesome! Bring me the gumi. I want to try."

We came up with all sorts of different tracks down the hill, but we always avoided The Drop-Off. It was the ultimate gumi challenge with great potential for pain and disaster. If taking the gumi on a track heading right over the drop-off wasn't difficult enough, after hitting the ledge you had about six feet before you ran into the large roots of a rubber tree.

The Drop-Off became one of those seemingly insurmountable obstacles of our childhood. Every day when we walked out of the house it stared at us waiting to be tried. Finally Landon was the first one to have the guts to challenge The Drop-Off. We pumped the gumi up until we thought it might burst to try to give him a little extra cushioning for his daredevil feat.

I stood at the top of the hill holding breath as Landon started rolling. Head over heels, Landon picked up speed aiming straight at The Drop-Off. His feet hit the ground right at the edge, and he pushed off with all his might. My whole body tensed as he catapulted skyward in what looked like slow motion. He did a half-rotation in midair while holding on to the gumi for dear life. This was not going to end well.

I watched in horror as he crashed back to earth and landed with a resounding thud upside down on his head. The gumi teetered and twisted like an out of control vehicle but somehow remained upright. With one final revolution Landon slid to a stop right at the base of the rubber tree. Mostly un-injured he climbed shakily out of the gumi and raised his hands in triumph. The Drop-Off had been defeated and a brand new X-games sport had been created. Landon was the gold medal winner.

Butterflies

I know that collecting butterflies isn't considered the "coolest" hobby these days, but that's because the butterflies here in America are rather drab. Papua New Guinea is home to some of the rarest, most beautiful butterflies in the world. These are not your average monarch butterflies. I'm talking about butterflies so large that when the first Australian explorers came to the island they named one species "Birdwings" because they shot down a specimen flying overhead so huge they thought it was a bird they could eat.

Whenever we traveled into the jungle, Dad brought his two butterfly nets with him. He and I were out in a remote village visiting translators when we emerged one afternoon with our nets in hand, ready for some fun. The national people were not quite sure what to make of us or our odd-looking nets. Curious to see what the strange whiteskins were doing, an assortment of village kids tagged along at a safe distance. There we were, two crazy Americans pushing through the undergrowth, hopping along streams in search of the perfect exotic butterfly with a gaggle of giggling kids chasing after us.

It didn't take long for the kids to figure out what was going on, and before you knew it they all spread out working as scouts. Suddenly our ragtag little group turned into a butterfly-finding machine. With large wings of rich royal blue, the most prized butterfly was called a Ulysses butterfly. They usually flew high up in the treetops, rarely landing within reach of our short nets.

One of the locals saw the Ulysses butterfly first and gave a shout. The magnificent specimen took off fleeing deeper into the jungle with us in hot pursuit. Leaping over large rocks and weaving in and out of trees, we tried not to lose our blue fluttering masterpiece.

I came to a halt, cradling my net like a lacrosse stick and feasted my eyes on the rare sight of the Ulysses butterfly sitting calmly on a wide green leaf as it sunned itself in a warm shaft of light. The kids were jumping up and down with excitement pointing at the butterfly. It was best if everyone kept still and silent so we didn't scare the butterfly away, but clearly that wasn't going to happen. Dad was in the rear, so I crept stealthily toward the unsuspecting sunbather. I inched closer and closer, afraid the slightest misstep would send the blue beauty flying. Barely breathing, I raised the army green net ever so carefully. The butterfly was within reach. Years of practice had led me to this exact instant. This was the moment of truth.

Of course, the butterfly happened to be in a most inconvenient spot for getting snagged in my net—he was shielded by a large branch underneath his leaf. The ideal scenario was to gently extend the open net below where he was sitting and then, with the snap of my wrist, come up underneath him, twisting the net once he was inside so he couldn't fly away. But that wasn't an option. I had to go for the side-swipe method.

My hands grew sweaty clenching the long metal neck of the net as I raised its open mouth. I took a deep breath. It was now or never. I struck with a swift swipe, raking my net across the leaf where the Ulysses was sitting.

As if he'd been toying with me the whole time only to make the anguish of defeat all the more painful, the butterfly flitted away just at the last second. I watched him disappear high into the jungle canopy and turned around to see a dozen or more disappointed faces staring back at me, but then somewhere nearby another butterfly was spotted and we were off racing through the jungle again.

My favorite butterfly story is a little unusual. One time after visiting a butterfly farm, my dad came home with two giant cocoons he had purchased. Inside these precious little sacks were Goliath Birdwing butterflies, which when hatched and mature, were the second biggest species of butterfly in the world. Dad built a fancy little mesh wall mount where he hung the cocoons, eagerly awaiting their emergence so he could add them to his collection. Weeks went by and we watched and waited, but the two small cocoons just hung there doing nothing.

My dad was nervous to leave them behind, but he had to go away on a trip for a week and leave my mother in charge of capturing the coveted butterflies should they choose to emerge in his absence. When I came home from school in the middle of the week, my mother was in a panic. "The damn butterflies are coming out!" she groaned. "Why couldn't your father be here for this?" Bugs weren't really her strong point, so that left me to take the lead. I was more than ready.

Fascinated, I watched them break forth from their cocoon and slowly climb up the wire mesh contraption Dad had built. When the butterflies first emerged their wings were still all curled up and wrinkly, so I had to let them unfold and dry out to their full size before I could capture them and put them into the freezer to die and then harden. Slowly their wings began to dry and unfurl, revealing giant wings speckled with beautiful deep black and canary yellow patterns, two sail-like appendages resembling two painted artists' canvases. Afraid to capture them prematurely lest they be ruined, I waited all afternoon, but they didn't seem to be in any hurry.

Having grown tired of hanging around watching the butterflies sunbathe, I stepped outside for a bit to shoot hoops. I'd barely walked out to the driveway when I heard yelling from back in the house. I ran indoors to find the larger of the two butterflies flapping furiously around the living room with my mother in hysterics. Apparently it had been waiting for me to leave before taking off. My mother is a wonderful Christian woman, but as the appropriately named Goliath butterfly flew around her head she unleashed an impressive string of words I never knew were in her vocabulary. The responsibility of capturing Dad's beautiful butterfly was too much for her. Using its newly acquired power of flight, the butterfly escaped down the hall flapping its way into my parents' bedroom. I chased after it, slamming the door behind me. I had the escapee cornered.

It landed on my father's bedside table flapping its wings back and forth as if mocking me. We'll see who has the last laugh, I thought. I grabbed the butterfly net but when I came back it was fluttering around the ceiling. Still as a statue, I stood with net in hand waiting for what felt like hours for it to land.

Mother poked her head inside the door to see how things were going. When she realized the butterfly was still at large, she let out a screech, closed the door and disappeared. She wanted nothing to do with the impending capture. At last our Goliath came back to earth. Sitting calmly in a patch of sunlight on the floor, it seemed oblivious to the tension it was causing. Tiptoeing around the bed, I crouched down and stared at its little black eyes. I spoke up. "It's only a matter of time really. One way or another I am going to get you, so let's do this the easy way."

Holding the bottom of the net with my left hand I gently lowered it over the Goliath butterfly, lulling my unsuspecting victim to sleep. When it finally fluttered upward to escape, it was too late. Victory was mine.

Dad usually handled the delicate part of extracting the butterfly out of the net without harming its wings. There is a little pressure point on a butterfly's body that temporarily paralyzes it if you squeezed the right spot. Hands shaking nervously, I gave it a squeeze through the net. It stopped fluttering. Perfect.

Shoot. I'd forgotten the glass jar to put it in. I ran down the hall, which was against house rules, and slid into the kitchen. Grabbing the first jar I could find, I dashed back. There was still no movement. Gently I reached under the net and picked up the Goliath, placing it delicately at the bottom. I sealed the lid and took a deep breath. My work here was done. I had just captured the biggest butterfly of my life. I placed the jar in the freezer and when Dad came home my mother made him swear he would not bring any more live cocoons into her house. And to his credit he never did.

Playing Tennis

I'm not sure how or why this family ritual started, but somewhere along the line it stuck. Every Sunday after church our little family of five headed to the tennis courts with rackets and water bottles in hand for a little friendly competition. My parents were not exactly expert tennis players, but they did their best to teach us.

We played on hard-surface tennis courts that were well past their prime and by now covered with cracks and loose debris. Every couple of shots the ball would take a nasty sideways skip or sometimes just never bounce at all. The courts were adorned with saggy nets and surrounded by a chicken wire fence filled with gaping holes. It was not unusual to have to pause the game because all but one of our balls had managed to squirt under or through the fence and roll far out of sight. When the balls didn't escape the premises they managed to disappear in the thick weeds growing all around the base of the fence, but those were not the last of our hazards.

When a shot was shanked on one side of the court and the ball careened up into the air, all five sets of eyes followed its arcing path, not daring to breathe as we waited to see if it would clear the makeshift fence. This was a regular occurrence for us, and too often our slow-motion tracking ended with the well-worn ball landing in the head-high grass growing out of the clogged drainage ditch. The green meteor would sink into the stagnant water just outside the court never to be seen again.

My older sister had absolutely no desire to be out playing tennis, let alone with her quirky family. She spent most of the time trying to sub out of the game or complaining about possible sunburn. Add to that my brother who at this point in his life was denying his innate competitive Harrar genes and spending most of the time goofing off, distracted by whatever little insects and creatures came across his path. Then of course there was me, so ridiculously competitive that I would take over the whole court and cry when I lost. There might have even been a couple racquet throwing incidents. I know that type of behavior might be hard to believe from a missionary kid, but believe it or not we are far from cherubs.

As we got a little older, things grew more interesting. One Sunday while we were playing I hit a forehand about as hard as I could right at my sister. When I close my eyes I can still see the scene as if it happened just yesterday:

I see Dreya standing frozen like a statue as the ball hones in toward her, heading directly for her face. There is the heavy crunch of the ball upon impact, and all of a sudden her plastic glasses snap in half and go skittering across the court. Dreya unleashes a blood-curdling scream as if she's been shot and is holding her face, tears running down her freckled cheeks.

Suddenly Dreya pulls herself away from focusing on her own pain long enough to stare daggers at me across the net. Then she yells as loudly as she can, "You meant to hit me!" Next thing I know, chaos breaks out. Mom and Dad are shouting. Andreya is still weeping as Mom runs over to try to comfort her. I'm apologizing as furiously as I can and have a sick feeling in my stomach that I'm about to be in really big trouble. Landon hops down out of the umpire chair smirking at me as he revels in the fact that I've managed to get myself into some hot water. Then he turns on his concerned face and applies a second layer of supporting arms to hug Dreya. Finally, the tears stop, the pieces of broken glasses are picked up and family tennis is over forever.

After her traumatic experience, my sister refused to play tennis anymore, and my parents decided it would be wiser for the sake of the family to find a new activity to do together, so we took up ping pong and Boggle.

I continued to play tennis on my own time and an old rain-warped backboard made of thin strips of bamboo became my faithful practice partner. The backboard was probably about 15 feet across and ten feet high. The ball never bounced straight off of the piecemeal backboard. Every hit was an adventure as the ball careened in all different directions after hitting the bamboo. Nonetheless, I loved it.

If I hit the ball over the backboard, which I did rather regularly, it flew into the high school. This was a significant problem because balls were expensive, and I usually had only one or two of them. The school was surrounded by a chain-link fence topped off with razor wire. I didn't want to walk all the way around to the regular school entrance to retrieve the balls, so I created my own little way in.

After I hit my last ball over, I exited the court through a small gate and walked with one foot on both sides of the small drainage ditch that ran between the outside of the tennis court and the steep bank, at the top of which stood the fence. During the rainy season this became a treacherous 50 feet of muddy terrain to maneuver before I arrived at my makeshift entry point. There was a natural low spot in the fence, and I conveniently dug just a little bit of the dirt out from under this section and bent up the lower half of the chain-link fence so I could squeeze underneath.

Before sneaking in I always had to do a quick check to make sure the ever watchful Mr. Holiday wasn't out and about. He had the ability to sniff out trouble and illegal activity before it ever took place, and he always seemed to show up at the most inconvenient times. When the coast was clear I'd slither under the fence to retrieve my errant shots. I probably spent as much time chasing balls as I did hitting them, but it didn't stop me from coming back.

Tennis became somewhat of an obsession for me. My grandfather in America would tape the finals of the Wimbledon and US Open tennis championships and send me the videos of the great matches between the likes of Pete Sampras and Andre Agassi and a host of my other tennis idols. I didn't have a coach, so I watched the videos over and over and tried to mimic their strokes when I hit the ball. As I hit against the backboard I imagined that I, in my chicken-wired, weed-infested tennis court on a South Pacific island, was in fact playing in one of the most beautiful stadiums in the world in front of raucous crowds. And of course, I was winning.

On Saturday mornings I used to get up at 7:00 a.m. to go join some of the missionaries to play doubles. It was my favorite time of the week. I loved the camaraderie and the competition against real people rather than the backboard and figments of my imagination.

One of my all-time favorite Saturday morning partners was Mr. Hong. He could barely speak a word of English, which made conversation rather challenging, but week after week we played together communicating through smiles and hand gestures and occasional "Ooooohs" when one of us managed to hit a decent shot. Somehow in spite of our language barrier we developed a deep connection, an unspoken bond of friendship between two people from two different worlds. Without words, he taught me the possibility of being a person of authentic humility and profound joy as he modeled this beautiful combination day in and day out.

During my junior year Mr. Hong found it necessary to return to Korea. At the end of our last possible Saturday tennis match we both stood on the court with our rackets dangling idly from our sides. There were a thousand things running through my head I wanted to say, but words were no good. There were no fancy good-byes or farewell speeches. Instead Mr. Hong broke the solemn silence by taking off the old Fox racing hat he wore every week. He dusted off his hat and handed it to me as a token of friendship by which to remember him. I bowed as I accepted it— and then gave him my bright red Phillies baseball hat in return. He smiled. We both put on our new hats and, with a final wave, went our separate ways.

I never saw Mr. Hong and his great smile again, but I like to think that somewhere in South Korea there is a red Phillies hat bobbing around on a tennis court. There with his effortless grace Mr. Hong is hitting his patented forehand. Someday in heaven we will partner again, but there we will speak the same language.

Community

It was 5:30 on a Friday afternoon and there were easily 100 hungry people waiting in line outside the big red building with chipping paint and thick rope hung across its front proudly spelling the words "Teen Center". The teen center was the only gig in town when it came to food, so it's no surprise that the missionary families from all over center brought their lawn chairs as they waited in the sprawling line for food. Like a hobbled centipede, the human chain slowly crept forward towards the ordering windows. We may have been serving burgers and fries, but it wasn't exactly *fast* food.

Soccer balls and frisbees buzzed overhead like bees and the poor family that owned the house across from the teen center watched as their yard was turned into a community field for whatever game was being played that week. If you listened closely you could overhear conversations in a multitude of languages from all over the world. Kids were running around like maniacs working up an appetite as they played every variety of tag imaginable, and teenagers were standing around trying to cut in line to join their friends now that they were too "cool" for the shenanigans of their younger siblings.

Every Friday this kaleidoscope of cultures and ages and activities ushered in the weekend. Inside, the walls only heightened the cacophony as people tried to find a seat at one of the wooden tables scattered haphazardly wherever there was floor space and covered with old red-and-white-checkered tablecloths straight out of the 1950s.

When working as a server I spent the whole night zigging and zagging through the crowds of people as I balanced food and drink orders and tried to spot the right set of faces to deliver them to. We didn't have any fancy beepers or pagers to notify people when their food was ready. It was just expected that you would know everybody who walked through the double doors of the teen center.

Now and again there were fresh faces in the crowd. New recruits just arrived from some far off place here to play their role in Bible translation. They were quickly welcomed into the community, and before long it was as if they'd always been there. Families returned from furlough and others left. It seemed that every plane either brought an old face back to us or took one away. The comings and goings were what bonded us. There was a sense of brevity to our life together, a need to squeeze the most out of every day. Time was short so we shared our lives deeply with one another, knowing that the plane to take us away would be coming far too soon.

Just inside the main entrance was a long ice cream counter furnished with high 3-legged stools. People would climb out of the river of young and old faces onto a stool for a brief respite as they waited for their food order to be processed. When I was the ice cream scooper on duty I doubled as the resident psychologist. I was a captive audience and all assortments of faces would appear ready to share about their week or their worries or whatever else was on their mind. Up to my elbows in ice cream and milk I just listened to their stories as the vintage milkshake machines whirred lazily in the background, and I did my best to keep up with the conversation and the orders for banana splits.

I watched sunburned and wrinkled faces, hard faces and soft faces. I listened as lips moved telling stories I could only begin to imagine and others shared experiences that struck close to home. Every face was different, but within the multitude of faces and stories was a beautiful commonality that drew us together. We were all ordinary people, sharing life together doing our best to love God and love our neighbors. Some days it was easy to love God and love our neighbor and those faces came shining and celebrating full of wonder and joy. But those days when the world made sense were balanced out by the days when loving God and loving neighbor seemed far beyond our grasp and those faces spoke with heavy words and drooping shoulders and weary eyes.

We were missionaries and missionary kids, but underneath the veneer of supernatural spirituality we were raw searching human beings; faces with hopes and dreams and heartache. Together our faces bore the image of Christ in their beauty and in their baggage. Together we were a community.

Water

In Papua New Guinea, when the rain showers hit our corrugated iron roof it sounded like thousands of tiny gunshots. And we were very resourceful; we didn't waste any water. All the rainwater ran down into gutters and filtered into a giant holding tank to become our drinking water. The tank looked like a small bomb shelter rising about six feet in the air. Made out of solid corrugated metal, it could hold a couple thousand gallons of water.

During the rainy season it didn't take long for the tank to fill to overflowing, but during the dry season we could go weeks at a time without rain.

One day Mom was mid-shower, all lathered up with soap and full of shampoo in her hair when the unthinkable happened. The faucet began to sputter. The water pressure dropped to a drip here and a drop there. And then nothing. The water stopped. Mom couldn't believe it. She yelled for my father to come help. Dad checked to make sure there wasn't an obvious problem with the plumbing. Everything looked fine. Mom was now standing wrapped in a towel waiting for good news with a head of shampoo suds.

Dad went outside to make sure everything was connected correctly. Yep. He found no issues there. The disappearance of the water was a mystery. One last thing to check: Dad went outside and tapped on the water tank. It sounded hollow—too hollow. He took a look inside. There was the problem. The tank was as dry as a bone! All the water was gone. Mom was not going to be happy. Dad had to drive her mid-shower to a friend's house so she could de-shampoo herself. It was the first time our family experienced running out of water, but not the last...

When I was a junior in high school my sister was a senior. Two of her close friends whose families had returned to the States permanently flew to PNG to live with us so they could finish out their last year in PNG with all of their old friends. And voilà, Valerie and Bekah arrived, turning our home into a dramatic, estrogen-filled soap opera. There were seven of us all together and it wasn't long before something became very obvious.

Dad called a secret meeting of the "men," and by "men" I mean Dad, my brother and me. Dad advised us that with the three teenage women in the house we were now going through water at an eye-popping and unsustainable rate. Unless drastic measures were taken, this was not going to end well. It was our duty to cut down on our water usage as much as possible. I took our water rationing to what I believed to be a healthy extreme. Each night when it was time to shower I took a plastic cup with me. I filled the cup up once to wet the washcloth and my hair. After lathering up with soap and shampoo, I then filled it up a second and final time to rinse off. Two cups.

One shower. Done! Now my brother, who was already going through a boyhood phase where he seemed to have become allergic to the combination of water and soap, took our water rationing to an unhealthy extreme. He began to go days at a time without a shower until the grime or the stench of his body drew too much attention. To him the whole thing was just a big game.

While we were cutting down on consumption, the three girls were doing their best to shower away our precious water as they preened and primped in the bathroom. Day by day I watched the water level in the tank dropping. Right smack dab in the middle of the dry season, there was no rain at all to pelt down on our roof, run into our gutters and refill our holding tank. At last the inevitable happened. To the mortification of the beautiful water guzzlers, we reached the bottom of the tank.

We had to switch our house over to unclean and at times visibly brown and murky river water. You can imagine how excited they were to be showering in this! There was no more drinking from the tap. Everything had to be filtered. Eventually the rains did come and the water tank filled up. The next time around everyone helped out with water conservation.

High Security

Living in PNG wasn't always a wonderful world of adventure. There were complicated cultural dynamics at play with some of our Papua New Guinean neighbors. Here the tale of Robin Hood can be helpful to us with its notion of robbing the rich to feed the poor. This was precisely the mentality we found. We were the rich and the neighboring people were the poor. We lived in nice Western houses while they lived in grass huts. We had plenty of clothes to wear and food to eat while the PNG people struggled to get by on very little. Wycliffe worked diligently to cultivate meaningful partnerships with local villages and provide education and job opportunities, but for a few trouble makers this was not enough.

While I was in elementary school armed men started breaking into houses on a nightly basis, and something had to be done. A night watch was set up with the missionary men patrolling the center all night until my 4th grade teacher, Mr. Kovach, was shot by the notorious bandit Minimus with a homemade gun. The whole center went on lockdown, and no one was allowed to leave their house because bands of men were roaming the center with machetes and flashlights.

Those were scary times, with whisperings that we might all have to leave. There was no police force ready to respond to emergencies. Heck, we didn't even have an emergency number we could call like 911. Instead, when there was danger or information that needed to be spread quickly, everyone was a part of a phone chain, and we would spread the news via our landline phones. The nearest cops with a vehicle were about 30 minutes away and weren't available most of the time, so there was no real outside help. We were on our own.

When we were home on furlough as kids, my sister dialed 911 to see if it worked like in the movies. When someone actually answered the phone she hung up immediately. Cool! A 911 call was real! This new revelation was much less cool when the cops showed up at the front door of our house shortly thereafter with guns and badges wanting an explanation for the call. Apparently they did not appreciate being a part of my sister's cultural education.

Eventually, the decision was made to erect a large chain link fence around the entire center for safety. A couple years after the fence went up, even greater precautionary measures had to be taken. An armed security firm called Guard Dog was hired to patrol the center 24 hours a day with their dogs and vehicles. On top of this, the entire center was put under curfew. If they saw anyone out after curfew, we feared the security people might release the dogs first and ask questions later.

One night under this stiff regime I found myself house-sitting for some friends and looking after their dogs. I confess I am not much of an animal lover, and when one of the dogs kept whimpering outside my door at two o'clock in the morning, keeping me from sleeping, I'd had enough. I stomped outside onto the porch to see what the problem was. Ah yes, they were out of water. How thoughtful of them to let me know so diligently. I refilled the bowl and was about to go back inside when I turned the door handle, only to realize that I'd locked myself out. I jiggled and shook the door as hard as I could to no avail. I stared at the dogs, now both laying calmly side by side. Dogs!

I could see my bed through the barred windows, but I couldn't get in. Gosh, freakin' dang it! (I made sure to use all the appropriate MK swearwords because obviously God didn't know what I really wanted to say.) It was a chilly night and I was in shorts and a T-shirt. I thought about running home at full speed and imagined the Guard Dog patrol car coming out of nowhere, and then behind me I imagined the baying of those vicious German Shepherds as they chased me down, tearing at my jugular. Maybe I should walk instead of run? Bad guys don't walk do they? They slink or sprint, but certainly not a slow stroll at two o'clock in the morning. I was nervous, but the thought of spending the next four hours or so until the sun came up freezing my behind off wasn't terribly compelling either. Finally I made up my mind.

Teeth chattering with nerves, I hopped over the backyard fence and scanned for guards or trucks. The coast was clear. I had to walk about a quarter mile to make it home. Scared out of my mind that I was about to be doggie chow, I half jogged, half ran my way across the center. Every nighttime sound made me jump, ready to scream, "I'm just a missionary kid. Hold your dogs!" By the time I arrived home my whole body was shaking in a flood of adrenaline. No guards. No dogs. I was safe. At least until I had to wake up my parents to let me into the house.

Playing Rugby

To most Americans, rugby is a strange international game where big burly men without pads gang tackle one another. The average viewer really has no idea what's going on between the kicking, backward passes and sideline throw-ins with guys getting lifted up into the air. Then of course there is the really odd stoppage of play when both teams lock shoulders and try to shove each other backward in what amounts to a massive group hug. Pretty quickly, the whole game is little more than a jumbled mass of chaotic activity. Interestingly, that's the opinion most of the world has about American football.

In Papua New Guinea, the people worship rugby. Even the most remote villagers are crazy about the sport. So, being a missionary kid there, learning to play was an essential part of growing up. Now you may have no idea how to play, but it doesn't take long to realize that rugby is not a sport for the faint of heart.

A group of us used to play rugby in my friend's side yard. It was a makeshift field if ever there was one. At one end, the end zone was the gravel road and at the other end it was a strip of trees and a big muddy drainage ditch. The field itself had its share of hazards, my favorite being the giant fern bush right at midfield! The poor fern took about as much punishment as the rest of us throughout the course of every game. Yet, like us, it somehow managed to stand the test of time. It was a survivor.

I stood waiting in my end zone for the opening ball to be kicked. It flew end over end through the air and then took a few awkward bounces before I could get my hands on it. I looked up at the boys advancing toward me at full speed and grinned. Let the games begin. With teammates on either side I charged forward, eluding the arms of the first tackler only to be walloped by the guy behind him. That was going to leave a bruise. As I was being dragged to the ground I flipped the ball backward to my teammate just before I ate a mouthful of grass.

He was tackled in the skinny section of the field between the bush and the neighbor's house. Not much space to dodge defenders there. He played the ball back to me and I tossed it to our third teammate. He chugged along, dragging defenders on both legs before he finally fell to earth like an enormous oak. I zipped in and snatched up the ball, darting past the last defender to score. It was Saturday, and there was no better way I could imagine to spend my day.

Over the years there were a lot of mud-stained shirts, bruises and skirmishes on our little strip of grass. There was glorious victory and devastating defeat. It was where we became men.

A special ingredient made for the best rugby playing: Mud! During the rainy season when it poured almost every day, mud wasn't too hard to find. Fearing we would turn the high school soccer field into a giant muddle puddle, the school's administrators banned us from using it to play rugby when it was wet. Now tell a bunch of high school boys what they aren't allowed to do and well…you know what's going to happen. The field was just too irresistible.

One particular time in the middle of the school day there was such a torrential downpour that the soccer field looked like an ocean as the wind whipped whitecaps from goal to goal. Without hesitation, those of us on study hall grabbed a ball and ran out onto the field. Before you knew it we had a full-fledged game of rugby going. Mud was the great equalizer; no matter how big or strong somebody was they could be tackled in the slippery mud.

Red, blue, gray… it didn't matter. After a few sliding tackles in the mud everything turned the same color. Arms and legs were painted a dark brown till we were one tribe of slippery howling mudmen. There we were, two lines of fearsome warriors charging each other at full speed. Feet churned in the mud. The ball carrier danced backwards and sideways before being dragged to the ground underneath a pile of flailing limbs. Somehow the ball popped out and was hurled across the field to waiting arms. Back and forth we raced slipping and sliding every step of the way. Out of nowhere, the PE teacher came storming out into the middle of the game yelling at us to stop.

We were all escorted down to the principal's office leaving behind a trail of muddy footprints in our wake. There were so many of us that we couldn't fit into the cramped office, so we stood outside and took our public scolding before being forced to write our names down on a piece of paper for future punishment. We proudly wrote down our names. Whatever they had in store for us, we had no regrets. We were from PNG and rugby was in our blood.

Swing Dancing

I was in 9th grade when the swing dance craze started. It was a bit of an undercover hush-hush sort of movement at first because "swing dancing" sounded far too sexual for some folks, mostly the old gray-haired missionaries. To them, just the thought of teenagers holding hands and moving rhythmically together smacked of the devil's work and next thing there would be babies out of wedlock. No dancing was allowed in any public buildings on the mission center to make sure everyone kept to the straight and narrow, but what happened on private property... well...that was fair game. So kids took to living rooms and basements, wherever they could find enough space.

My first time going to dance my hands were shaking with excitement and nerves as I trudged up the steep hill following the red dirt road. When I finally arrived at the right place I was surprised to see it was just the shell of a house still under construction with floors that were barely nailed down. I stepped out of the dark night and into the swirling world of swing. People were weaving and spinning around piles of building materials, and I could look out through skeletal walls and see the outline of grass-covered hills underneath the blaze of a million stars.

I immediately fell in love with the music, but the whole "dancing with a girl" thing I wasn't so sure about. I stood on the outside and found my feet tapping vigorously to the beat. It was all a little overwhelming as partners careened about and from time to time went flying in the air with billowing skirts filled up like parachutes.

I was late. The tutorial session for beginners was already over. There seemed to be an endless number of moves to learn as people spun this way and that, yo-yoing past each other, somehow knowing exactly what they were supposed to do as if by telepathy. Of course not everybody seemed to have this telepathic connection. The newbies were not hard to spot as they awkwardly shuffled their feet back and forth, every now and again venturing into something a little more complicated, only to return to the basic awkward shuffling and staring at feet.

I was glued to the wall when one of the older girls broke protocol and asked me to dance. She was tall and I was short. She knew what she was doing and I didn't have a clue. I was nervous and she was not. Everything was backwards, but somehow it worked.

She steered me onto the floor and showed me how to place my hands. Hers were the first female hands I had ever held outside of my own family or some sort of prayer circle. It was strange. I had always shied away from these sorts of interactions.

"Step together. Step together. Rock Step," she called out, trying to describe what I was supposed to be doing with my feet, pulling me gently to the left and to the right with her hands. Eventually that part would be my job. I tried desperately to keep up. Slowly and simply she kept reminding me. Little by little I began to figure it out, and after a couple of songs I stopped thinking about the fact that I was holding a young lady's hand.

After much coaching and plenty of mistakes I finally learned how to do a basic turn, which in all honesty is not exactly a glorious life achievement, but it sure felt like it at the time. My poor partner had to duck every time she passed under my outstretched arms while I stood on my tippy toes wishing I were taller.

When a good half hour had gone by we started getting sophisticated and attempted "the pretzel," which is about as complicated a dance move as the name would suggest, with a whole lot of spinning and twisting and tangled arms. She ducked under my arm and, having to stoop so low while trying to wriggle out of the jumbled mess we'd managed to make of ourselves, ended up on the floor, bringing me down with her. We collapsed in a heap amongst the sawdust. She laughed. I laughed. This was fun. Little by little, dance after dance, she helped me until we were really swinging. By the end of the night we even managed to conquer the pretzel without any casualties.

After that I was hooked. We started holding dances once a month. Somewhere along the way a formal petition was passed allowing us to swing dance in public buildings. Apparently after the overly-protective parents came and saw what was *really* going on, they decided maybe the devil hadn't seized our rebellious teenage minds to lead us astray. Soon afterward we started using the Teen Center. Before we knew it, we had a packed house.

An expected social etiquette arose to govern the dancing scene: Girls waited to be asked and guys were expected to do the asking. We were rather traditional in this regard. This always made for an interesting dilemma: All the guys sat together in a clump trying to ignore the stares from the gaggle of girls across the room, and an awkward tension hung in the air between the two groups. This tension was only magnified because there were always more girls than guys who showed up to dance. As a guy, if you sat out a couple dances in a row, the annoyed looks might turn to death stares.

If you weren't "officially" dating someone, you had to be careful about whom you chose as a partner and how often you danced with a partner. If you danced too many times with the same girl in one night, people might have thought you were interested in her. It didn't take much for rumors to spread. Two long dances close together could be the unsuspected beginning of a romance neither party wanted or, even worse, only one party did. God forbid you should hold somebody in the "cuddle" position for too long. There were always eyes watching and social undercurrents at work beneath the dancing feet. But that didn't stop me. By the end of every evening I'd head home drenched in sweat from dancing all night with as many partners as I possibly could. I loved it.

Fast forward a year, and I found myself looking in the mirror feeling rather uncomfortable in my oversized black suit. Brown hair loaded with gel continued to rebel in spite of my best efforts. My date, Anna Proper, would be here any minute along with the rest of our homecoming crew. This was my first American school dance. It was to be an experience unlike any other.

The evening started off with pictures, far too many pictures. We decided to keep it classy so we went to Ruby Tuesday for the pre-dance dinner. One enormous bowl of French onion soup later, I was a man on a budget; it was time to get our dancing on. The gym parking lot was filled with classy cars and couples strolling in fancy suits and scandalous dresses. At least *I* thought they were scandalous. No one else seemed bothered by the amount of skin on display. The scandal was just beginning.

We stepped into the gym, all decorated with streamers and balloons. The lights were turned down low and pop music was blasting. As my eyes adjusted to the darkness I suddenly felt sick to my stomach. This was not about to be a swing dance party. People were bumping and grinding and doing "devil" dancing as the old missionaries called it. If only they could have seen this.

The music, deafening, it was nearly impossible to hold a conversation. Clearly the point of the night was not to get to know your date through verbal communication. I slipped into a seat at one of the tables along the wall as my date disappeared into the fray, and I wouldn't see her again all night. I naively believed that I had come to swing dance.

What about Grace?

Growing up in Papua New Guinea had its shadow side. The small community created the sort of environment where everybody knew each other's business. Wherever you went people were always observing you, and by that I mean, yes, even missionaries are a little bit too nosy for their own good at times. Missionaries tend to have high moral expectations both for themselves and for their kids. This sort of comes with the territory. When missionaries return home they are viewed as spiritual giants and heroes who have given up the conveniences of an easy modern life to suffer and do God's work abroad. Now it would be difficult and rather unhealthy enough if these lofty expectations were placed only on mature Christian missionaries. Sadly, these same pressures are placed upon the shoulders of MKs who, like most other young people, are in the midst of the delicate process of finding themselves, which is difficult enough without everyone around them watching their every move in case they step out of line.

As a result, we often weren't really allowed to be kids. We were expected to behave like miniature adults. It was drilled into us to work hard at school, play an instrument and know our Bibles backward and forward. Parents and teachers placed a great deal of emphasis on performance and the external. There was very little leeway for students to make mistakes.

If you acted out too much, your whole family could be asked to leave the mission field. This pressure made parents crack down on their kids.

The community pressed its values and expectations upon us. We were given the beat to march to, and God forbid if we should try to march or dance to our own beat! It often felt like we were created to be cookie-cutter Christians who looked, thought and acted the same. There was little room for ambiguity. The world was staunchly black and white, and those who saw it in shades of gray found themselves in a lot of trouble or quickly learned just to be quiet.

In this highly educated, child-focused community with few outside distractions, there was a constant sense of competition. Mediocrity was not an option; it was despised like a disease. As a naturally competitive person, I thrived in this environment. I studied more and practiced longer (for sports, not for my trumpet, that is) than the rest of my peers. I became addicted to the praise of man. I became obsessed with getting all As and hearing my name called at awards ceremonies. The more attention I received the more it fed my addiction.

I became the missionary poster child. I did it all. I was class president, a good student, a singer on the worship team and more. I desperately wanted to prove myself and please the adults around me. I based my entire identity on what I could do and what I achieved. Every test was nerve racking. Every trumpet audition was laden with stress. I couldn't sleep before sports tournaments. I was scared to death of failure.

So, after years of church and Sunday School, I didn't have a clue about grace. Yes, I could define it for you and give you many Bible references that talked about it, but I didn't understand it. My relationship with God was one of guilt. As much as I tried, I couldn't be perfect. While I hid my insecurities and fears and shortcomings from the world, I knew God saw me for who I really was: a scared young man weighed down by internal and external expectations. I was always striving to do better, trying to read my Bible more and pray longer without falling asleep. I worked to earn God's approval and acceptance the same way I did with the adults in my life. In the same manner I was motivated by a desire to win awards, I was driven in my spiritual journey by a need to hear God say, "Well done, my good and faithful servant." To me, God was a God of discipline.

After 17 years of frantic work, I graduated at the top of my class and left for college on a scholarship. Back in America, away from my little world of 1500 people, I still found myself competing at everything in life. I had to win. I had to be the best. I had to prove myself. When I messed up I showered myself with guilt because that's what I'd been taught. Failure was not an option. I promised God I would do better, and I worked even harder to make up for my earlier mistakes. On the outside I looked great because of this rigorous work ethic and impeccable moral standard. I was a kid who was going places, but inside it was never enough. I was always lacking. I lived that way, stuck in the unrelenting grasp of works righteousness, until God finally broke through in the most unexpected way.

I can't really say I found grace. Actually, grace found me! And there's something very fitting about that. I graduated from college and had just started dating an amazing young woman named Alison. One night after a date, I was about to head home and the two of us were standing at the end of her driveway with the stars twinkling as the lovely smell of Lancaster manure wafted through the air ruining every ounce of romance. Right there in that moment Alison said the thing that changed my life forever. I cannot remember the context of the conversation, but she looked at me with great intensity and said, "Simeon, I don't love you because of all the different things you can do and have achieved in your life. I love you for who you are."

I stood there with a deer-in-the-headlights look, dumbfounded. How could she say such a thing?! Just like that, she'd taken all of my years of stockpiling trophies, awards and gold stars and thrown them in the trash. They were not important to her. They did not define me. I watched all my efforts slide away into the abyss, all those things I thought would be necessary to earn her approval and make her love me. I thought I would woo her with my sports skills and trumpet-playing and report card prowess. But none of those things mattered. I was more than the sum total of my external achievements.

I wept big ugly tears the whole way home that night as the reality began to sink in. I began to name the things I was so proud of and gave them up—praying well in public, reading my Bible, spotless church attendance. The list kept going until I stood naked before God. I had nothing to offer. All of the things I'd been dragging before God for years to try to impress Him were discarded. And there in that moment Jesus dealt the first blow to my addiction, and grace began to flow. Grace ran like a river through my parched and weary soul, and at last healing could begin.

Chapter 2
Foreign Holidays

My parents did their best to prepare us for life in America. Part of this preparation meant that as a family we attempted to carry out typical American traditions and holidays. It was bad enough my parents stole us away from our extended family, but to have taken us away and turned us into uncultured savages, well that would have been an unforgivable sin. It was my parent's duty to turn us into well-mannered American citizens, and by golly against great odds they gave it their best effort.

Gingerbread Houses

We built our first family Gingerbread house in Senegal, Africa to get in touch with our American roots and, in true Harrar fashion, we went all out. Mom and Dad made everything from scratch, rolling and measuring the gingerbread to form the different pieces of the house. Mom had managed to bring some of my grandmother's old metal cookie cutters of all different shapes and sizes to Senegal, and we put them to good use.

We kids went to work stamping out reindeer and gingerbread men and Christmas trees and then impatiently waited for them to cook in the oven. The oven was nearly unnecessary in the brutal African heat turning our little home into a sauna. As our creations cooled down we tried to steal the pieces of candy meant for eyes and the shredded coconut to be sprinkled on for hair or a set of bushy eyebrows. These rare delicacies did not appear often in our house, so we couldn't contain ourselves. At last the gingerbread cooled down and we were unleashed to dip and drizzle and spread icing to our heart's content.

My father meticulously used the icing as mortar to hold all the parts of the gingerbread house together. There were a few broken toothpicks shoved in here and there for good measure until the house stood on its own, a true work of art and a monument to

American Christmas festivities. We slopped white icing down for snow and slathered all the other colors on the walls of the house till it looked like a piece of Jackson Pollock artwork. We strategically placed gingerbread men in and around the house and we made sure Frosty the Snowman was prominently displayed in the front yard. Dad even made icicles to hang from the roof. It was a masterpiece so perfect, in fact, that we were afraid to touch it, let alone eat it.

Shortly after our work of art had been placed proudly on display, we were mortified to walk in and discover the heads had been mischievously munched off all the gingerbread men, including our fat Santa preparing to somehow make his way down the skinny chimney. The decapitator crossed religious lines when not even gingerbread Jesus in the manger was spared. It was an outrage! Who could have done such a thing! No one confessed guilt, leaving only one option.

The culprit was none other than my baby brother Landon. Left by himself for just a minute, he apparently took a liking to gingerbread with his newly cut teeth and, in a flurry of crumbs, his irreparable work was done. And with that…Merry Christmas to all and to all a good night!

Awkward Christmas

Christmas for our missionary family was not your average Christmas. For starters, we lived on a tropical island, so all those songs about having a white Christmas and sledding through the snow really meant nothing to us. Our precipitation options started and ended with rain. So while the 80-degree heat and lack of a fireplace made it a little difficult to get into the Christmas spirit, we still tried our best.

Every year we put up the same fake scraggly Christmas tree and covered it in all sorts of ornaments from around the world. We had the set of heirloom Christmas balls my father received from his grandfather and had carted across the globe with him. Then, of course, there were boxes and boxes of homemade craft ornaments composed of anything from colored yarn to dried noodles. Throw on some colored lights and cover everything in a thick layer of silver tinsel and presto, you have the classic Harrar tree.

Come December 25th, the big X-factor was how many presents would be under the tree. It could take months for packages and presents to make the long journey to PNG, especially when shipped by boat. So unless friends and family were thinking way ahead of the game, there was no telling exactly when their presents would arrive. Some years there were piles of presents waiting under the tree on Christmas morning. On other occasions it was rather slim pickings. The upside to this was that we sometimes had Christmas all year round because the presents kept arriving. We just never knew when we might come home from school to find a freshly arrived package waiting to be unwrapped. Merry Christmas in July!

We were blessed to have lots of churches and supporters who sent us gifts. Now while this was great, it also provided some interesting moments. Not every kind-hearted Christian saint knows how to give age-appropriate gifts. There was nothing worse than opening a highly anticipated present you'd been staring at and shaking for weeks, only to find it filled with underwear or toothbrushes.

In that moment we weren't allowed to show our disappointment because Mom and Dad would videotape us opening the presents so we could send a tape of our excited faces and gushing thank-yous back to the church. We did our best to play the part and gave some award worthy performances over fresh soap and socks. Don't tell anyone, but if our acting wasn't quite up to snuff we would just re-wrap the gift and do a second take.

To add another interesting wrinkle to the whole experience, we were always advised to do our best to save the wrapping paper because it was hard to come by. Year after year we saw the same patterned paper recycled when my mother wrapped gifts. Apparently Santa was into recycling. One year when we were home in the States, we celebrated Christmas at my grandparents' house. I received the first gift to open. I began to carefully undo the bow and slowly peel off the tape on the corners of the box. This was some pretty sweet wrapping paper, and I was sure Santa would want to use it again. My grandmother looked at me as if I were losing my mind. "Just rip the paper!" she said.

My eyes opened wider and wider as I began to comply with my grandmother's wishes—it was against the rules. I felt my fingers begin to shake nervously. With great guilt I tore off the paper, expecting something terrible to happen as I did. Much to my surprise no warning alarms went off. In fact, it was kind of fun.

Every year around Christmas our little missionary store would receive a shipment of seasonal goodies like candy canes and fancy chocolates from America. This was always a big deal because there was really nowhere else to go shopping for gifts. On the day of the special Saturday Christmas sale, the only time of the year the store was open on the weekend, there would be a line of people waiting for the doors to open. There were two separate shopping periods, one for the women and one for the men, so spouses could buy each other gifts without the other knowing. The women were allowed to shop first one year and the men the next year.

When it was our turn, I joined the crowd of men rifling through all of the new arrivals. With my meager savings weighing heavily in my pocket, I searched high and low for inexpensive treasures. I walked up and down the aisles overwhelmed by what seemed like an endless array of options. I mean, there were three different kinds of candy canes and many different boxes of assorted chocolates. How was I ever supposed to make such a difficult decision? It was all just too much for me. I would be sure of something and put it into my little shopping basket only to return it a few minutes later when I found something else that tickled my fancy. I went back and forth, agonizing over each item, returning items time and time again only to put them back into my basket on my next trip by. Finally, when my precious bills were sweaty and wrinkled from being counted and recounted, I made up my mind. Excitedly I'd return home on a shopper's high, trying my best not to spill the beans on what I'd purchased for everybody.

The first time we were home on furlough and I was old enough to go Christmas shopping, I had a rude awakening. First, it was bitterly cold outside and we couldn't find a parking space close to the mall entrance because of all the shoppers, so we ended up parking about a half mile away. I'd just barely started to warm up in the back seat since the heat in our car was temperamental and miserably slow, when I had to clamber back out into the freezing temperatures. The cold wind cut right through my coat. I guess it was "Jack Frost nipping at my nose," but it felt like Jack was attempting to bite my face off. We ran most of the way to the entrance and nearly smacked into the automatic doors as they took their time opening up.

Then, as we skidded into the mall, I couldn't believe my eyes. There was not just one store, but store after store after store. There were more aisles than I could count filled with potential Christmas presents. Even the walkways were crowded with vendors selling Christmas junk out of carts, as if the regular stores weren't enough. My eyes bounced back and forth between all the beautiful window displays, like watching a long tennis point, as I tried to take everything in. All the brightly colored SALE signs made my head spin. There were no sales in PNG and no coupons. You always paid the price marked. It was simple.

There was an entire store dedicated to selling chocolates! I had never dreamed of such a thing. As I stared through the glass at the endless rows of fudge, truffles and gooey filled options, I knew I'd never be able to choose one kind to buy for my mother. The department store where I went in search of perfume for my sister was no better. Bottle after bottle, name brand after name brand, all sat in their sophisticated bottles way beyond my price range. I couldn't believe how expensive perfume was. Maybe if my sister wanted one present for the next decade I could afford to buy her one of these strange-smelling scents. We went to "Bath and Body Works," where things seemed more affordable. I finally found something, but when my father realized how long the line was he refused to wait. I couldn't blame him. It hardly seemed worth it for such a tiny purchase. So out we went, empty handed.

The whole experience was so overwhelming we decided to leave. I didn't buy even one item. I just wanted to go back to my little store where life was simple.

An American Thanksgiving

Our family was once invited to the 4th of July party at the American Embassy in Senegal. When we arrived, my sister and I made a mad dash for the table covered in delicious American delicacies. We were not interested in the deviled eggs or the pumpkin pies. With all the dignitaries watching, we ran to the hors d'oeuvre tray, and with squeals of delight shoved as many black olives as we could onto all of our fingers, while stuffing dill pickles in our mouths and waggling them about like cigars. We sprinted to my parents, sucking the olives off our fingers with extravagant lip-smacking that reverberated around the party.

Mom and Dad were trying to hide amongst the well-dressed crowd and pretend they didn't know us, but it didn't take long for us to spot them. They stuck out like the olives on our thumbs in their well-worn missionary attire. At the top of our lungs we shouted, "Look, Mom: Olives!" There was a lot of snickering and more than a few comments like, "Well, it's not hard to tell who the missionary kids are." My parents were extremely patriotic as they blushed a deep shade of red.

With this experience playing in the back of their minds and the fear of how we me might behave in front of our families when we next returned to America, my mother and father thought it would be a good idea for us kids to have a traditional American

Thanksgiving experience. They concocted the idea of purchasing a live turkey and fattening it up a couple of months ahead of Thanksgiving, which is not exactly a nationally celebrated holiday in Senegal.

My father, who has a wonderfully adventurous spirit, hopped into our little white station wagon built in Turkey, and rode to the crowded bird market on the other side of the city. After haggling and bargaining like only he can do, he came home with the scrawniest live turkey you have ever seen. Our small court yard became the white turkey's new home. Apparently my father did not make quite as good a deal as he had thought. It seems the seller of the bird knew something about this particular bird that allowed him to sell it at such a "good" price. You see, my father managed to purchase the oddest turkey that ever lived in the Dakar desert. First of all, the turkey decided its primary task in life was to poop everywhere. Now this was fascinating because the stupid turkey refused to eat everything my parents tried to feed it—except for lettuce. As you can imagine, a diet of lettuce and water and a healthy dose of pooping is not the ideal formula for fattening up a holiday bird.

Somehow my sister and I fell in love with the turkey, in spite of its quirkiness, during its stay in the courtyard. We named it Tom—Tom the turkey. One day my dad went out to the courtyard and found a beautiful white egg, a turkey egg. It turned out that Tom was really Thomasina. There was something devastatingly cute about Tom. The skinny fowl became our new pet and our favorite feathered friend. Thanksgiving arrived and much to my mother's frustration, that "damned" turkey, as she affectionately referred to it, weighed only a little over five pounds. She had invited a large number of African guests to come and join in our American Thanksgiving festivities and was now forced to go out and buy a slew of chickens to feed everyone.

But don't think the turkey got off the hook! No, my father made sure of that. He took my sister and me and poor spindly Tom down to the beach. To this day I have no idea why he thought it would be a good idea for us to come and witness what was about to take place. We stood and watched as he stuck Tom's head into the sand and, with one swift chop, severed his neck, letting the dark red blood run into the sand. As if that weren't enough, he then proceeded to pluck the gnarly little bird right in front of us so it would be ready to cook.

The trauma was far from over. Back at home, my sister and I sat and stared at the oven as what was left of our five-pound friend cooked to a crisp, golden brown. To top it off, we were then told politely to eat the bony guy along with our mashed potatoes and gravy. No wonder neither of us to this day likes the taste of turkey; and so much for the typical American Thanksgiving!

Chapter 3
Travel Stories, GPS Not Included

"See the world," they said. "Travel to exotic places. Fly across magnificent oceans and experience the most amazing marvels that culture and creation have to offer!" But what they really meant was this…

"Enjoy the airports of the world. Get lost en route to strange places. Sit in terminals for hours on end and experience the amazing power of jet lag and culture shock."

Taxi Taxi

Every four 4 years we faced our true American culture exam as we headed back to the United States on furlough, but before we got there we had to survive the trip.

On one occasion our exhausted family at last managed to find our way to the taxi line in the Hong Kong Airport. Dressed in our four-year-old, non-matching attire that screams "Missionaries!" we wind our way through the enormous snaking queue of travelers dragging our ten pieces of luggage and carry-ons with us. We finally get to the front of the line where a man who speaks no English is dressed in a delightful black suit with buttons and a throwback chauffeur's hat. He is directing the mob of taxis that are also waiting in line to pick up passengers. He looks at us and our lumpy suitcases and holds up two fingers: two taxis. My father shakes his head and raises a single finger: one taxi. The man shakes his head back, re-emphasizing the two fingers. This little discussion is going nowhere, and there is not a chance my father is about to pay for two taxis.

A jumpy Yellow Cab driver pulls up without permission and gets out of his car. He and the traffic director start chattering back and forth. The taxi driver shakes his head yes: one taxi. He walks around to the back of his trunk and pulls out a ball of bungee cords. This is about to get interesting. By the time the taxi driver and my father were finished, the trunk was hanging open in the back with suitcases sticking out, while bags were piled to the ceiling on the inside. I'm sure it wasn't legal, but somehow they made everything fit. It was nothing short of a miracle.

In the midst of the packing frenzy I was carefully stuffed into the only available space—I found myself curled up in a ball in the foot space behind the front passenger's seat. I couldn't see anything because I was covered by a giant 50-pound suitcase along with a small pile of carry-ons. The taxi driver was not running the AC, so I was simultaneously suffocating and drowning in a puddle of my own sweat while being slowly crushed to death by the mountain of luggage. Weaving in and out of traffic as dangerously as we did through the busy Hong Kong streets, even the most laid back individual would go into cardiac arrest with the constant horn-honking and lane-shifting. Somewhere up above me my mother, sister and brother were stacked three laps high in the space meant for a single person. Dad was traveling first class, sitting up front all by himself with his feet stretched out.

You should have seen the looks on the faces of the hotel staff when we arrived at our destination. They couldn't believe what they saw—passenger after passenger kept piling out of the vehicle, along with more and more luggage. It was like something out of a Harry Potter movie. And that, folks, is how we missionaries roll!

The Two-Suitcase Rule

All of our traveling meant that I spent most of my life under what I call the two-suitcase rule. It's a very simple rule. Whenever you move you are allowed to bring two suitcases along with you, and each suitcase must weigh less than 50 pounds. Any other earthly possessions that didn't fit into those two bags were left behind.

The two-suitcase rule came into play time and time again when we moved. If something didn't fit, it was given away. I could pack everything I owned in life into two suitcases in less than 30 minutes. I considered that a badge of honor. Life was simple when lived according to the two-suitcase rule.

My freshman year of college I showed up with the two-suitcase rule in full effect. I could hardly believe my eyes when I walked into my dorm room and saw how much stuff my roommate had. Thanks to him our room had a microwave, mini fridge, TV and lots more. The walls on his side of the room were covered in posters and pennants, and his desk was littered with all sorts of cool knickknacks.

My roommate, Jimmy, looked at my two wobbly suitcases and offered to help me bring in the rest of my stuff from the car. "Oh, thanks but this is all I have." He looked at me like I was kidding. Clearly he was equally surprised by my lack of stuff. Nobody had told him about the two-suitcase rule.

The two-suitcase rule had its strengths and weaknesses. On the positive side it forced you to live simply and really consider what things were important to you. On the other hand, it was a nightmare for my parents when we got ready to go overseas.

Imagine trying to pack everything you need for four years into just two 50-pound suitcases. Add in the fact that we were going to a country with no malls or other major retailers, the closest quality clothing store was an entire country away, and it would take six to ten weeks for somebody to ship us a package from home at the cost of their first born child. Sounds bad? Well, it gets worse: Now multiply this tension by five for each member of our family, and throw in three little kids who are going to do some serious growing over the next four years for which you have to anticipate and pack!

I watched Mom and Dad pack and repack, hoisting the suitcases on and off the groaning scale amidst Dad's grunts and the occasional curse. Ratty zippers and Dad's back threatened to break until all the bags hit the magic number—50. The easy part was now complete.

When our van pulled up at the airport curb we exploded out the door like a swat team. Everyone knew the drill. Carry-ons and fanny packs were tightly secured as the massive unloading began. Some pulled, some stacked, some guarded. With carts stacked five suitcases high like miniature Leaning Towers of Pisa, people stared in amazement as we made our grand entrance. When we had to pay for carts, we avoided the cost and just pulled the suitcases along on their own wheels and were an even more impressive sight to behold—like a fleet of ships moving together in formation. People quickly got out of the way of our ten squeaky suitcases, watching in wonder as we three kids huffed and puffed pulling suitcases that weighed about as much as we did, if not more. Between us and our army of luggage, we took up practically an entire baggage check line.

Things always started off well, but after we encountered a couple of slow-moving lines, the excitement of traveling started to wear off, and the three youngest Harrars began to grow restless and consider mutiny. And when the sleep deprivation and jet lag began to kick in during the multiple-day journey halfway around the world through 18 time zones, our once high-flying fleet turned into a bedraggled mess.

We became the awkward family sprawled out on the airport floor everyone stares at as they walk by. We didn't care. Fanny packs and wrinkled track jackets turned into pillows and blankets. We marked out our territory with backpacks, discarded shoes and the strong smell of body odor.

To this day I don't know how my parents did it. Attempting such a wild trip once would be one time too many for most folks. My parents made the trek every four years! Suddenly life in the South Pacific doesn't seem quite so appealing.

One time on our way back to America we had an 18-hour layover in Hong Kong. The thought of trying to keep us kids entertained in the airport for that long was just too much for them, so Mom and Dad splurged on getting us into a VIP travel lounge. This was a once-in-a-lifetime deal. When we made our way into the upscale lounge, filled with men and women in fashionable business suits reading newspapers, it became immediately clear that we were the oddballs. Mom and Dad didn't care. The lounge was equipped with internet access, a fancy leather massage chair and an unlimited supply of ice cream. All three of us kids were in heaven.

We spent the next 18 hours hopping from the computers to the massage chair to the mini fridge stocked with pints of Häagen Dazs® ice cream. I'm not sure how much it cost Mom and Dad for us to stay in that lounge, but I guarantee you that I personally ate enough ice cream to cover the cost of admission. To this day I can't see a Häagan Dazs® ad or a massage chair without recalling that experience.

A less pleasant memory took place during another trip back to America. I was sitting in my airplane seat for the eight-hour flight to Singapore, where we were going to be visiting friends for the next couple of days, when I began to feel very itchy. I advised my mother of the itching and she told me not to worry about it, I was probably just having allergies or something. Easy for her to say—she wasn't the one itching all over! The itching was unbearable, but at 30,000 feet there was nothing I could do. A small serving of delicious airplane food and in-flight entertainment did help a little, but the itching was definitely getting worse, not better.

We arrived in Singapore at some ungodly hour and made our way to our friends' 9th-floor apartment with no air-conditioning. Even in the early morning you could feel the thick heat bearing down. Unable to take the itching any more, I ran into the guest room and tore off my shirt and started scratching like a maniac. Andreya walked in and screamed. My whole back and stomach were covered in red spots. I had somehow managed to contract chicken pox on the plane. Imagine how my mother felt when she found that out!

Things would only get worse. It was illegal to go outdoors in Singapore if you have the chicken pox, so for the next four days I sat indoors in the sweltering heat with a pathetic little ceiling fan churning overhead while I watched reruns of Ben Hur in Chinese on our friends' tiny television.

While I was trapped upstairs without calamine lotion or a bath to soak in to ease my misery, my family was busy going around the city seeing all the magnificent sights of Singapore. On the hottest day of our visit, in an act of sheer cruelty, they ditched me to go down to the beautiful blue pool directly below our 9th-floor apartment. From the window I could make out their little figures diving and swimming in the cool crystal water. The real low moment came when they tried to bring me a spool of cotton candy, but by the time they got to the apartment the whole thing had melted and all that remained was a sticky pink blob on a paper tube, a shadow of its former sugary glory.

When it came time to leave, my parents dressed me in long pants and a jacket with a baseball hat pulled low over my face. Apparently it is also illegal to *leave* the country if you have chicken pox, so there I was sweating and itching to death in the sweltering heat while my parents illegally smuggled me out of the country so we didn't miss our flight. If you ever mention Singapore around me and I start to itch uncontrollably or instantaneously blurt out a swearword or two, you will now understand and, hopefully, have the heart to forgive me.

The Station Wagon

When we finally arrived in America for our yearlong furlough the traveling had just begun. There were thousands of miles to be driven all across the country visiting family and friends supporters. My grandpa always had a car waiting for us to use for these cross-country treks. This would not be just any car. Whatever car it was, it would somehow have managed to pass the meticulous Frank Harrar inspection, which was no easy feat. My grandpa is not a man of many words and is not quick to show his emotions, but preparing a reliable car was his little way of letting us know he loved us even when we were a world away.

On more than one occasion the highly anticipated vehicle awaiting us was none other than a wood-paneled station wagon. Oh yes, we received the station wagon in the height of its mid-90s heyday when for some terrible reason America thought wood paneling was a good idea. Just go back and watch some 90s music videos and you will realize how off kilter we were as a country. That wonderful wood-paneled wagon, piled to the roof with luggage, became our home away from home as we crisscrossed the country visiting friends, relatives and supporters.

Let me now take a few minutes to break down all of your preconceptions about MKs being perfect little cherubs. My brother, sister and I ditched our halos for pitchforks as soon as we had to choose seats. If Mom sat my younger brother, Landon, and me together it was only a matter of minutes before we were attacking each other, doing our best impression of the hulk smash or a ninja turtle maneuver. I was usually the victor while my brother ended up in tears, but he got his revenge when I was scolded for picking on him.

The other alternative was to put my older sister, Dreya, in the middle seat to separate us boys. Much to my parents' consternation, we would telepathically call a cease-fire against each other and gang up on Andreya. Poking and prodding, we annoyed her as much as we could until she burst into tears and was covered in bruises. In our defense, she bruised easily!

When all hell broke loose, my father pulled the car over and then we knew we were in trouble—well, mostly me, because I was the oldest instigator of treason and mutiny and therefore bore the greater responsibility. At least that's what Mom and Dad always claimed. Mom would then move to the back and sit between us two boys watching us like a hawk while Dreya got the front seat all to herself. Of course, Landon and I thought this was terribly unfair, so we whined and complained, but to no avail. If purgatory is real, then I will assuredly be doing some serious time for my role in all the shenanigans that took place in that old station wagon. Here I make my public declaration of guilt and beseech my parent's forgiveness.

When secluding my sister in the front wasn't enough or when my mom was tired of being the target of our constant squirming, kicking and complaining, there was one final option. The station wagon had a rather unique feature that came in handy. The back floor of the trunk folded up and there, hidden underneath, was a small, isolated seat. So as you can see, my parents were not above solitary confinement. You knew you'd really crossed the line when you were banished to the trunk seat. There was usually a wall of luggage between you and the rest of the car, so you had no idea what was going on as you stared out the back window.

My parents did have a couple of tricks up their sleeves to keep us quiet and cooperative. The first was food. They used to buy bags of those rounded rice cakes that look and taste like cardboard. Throw in some Snyder's beer pretzels, the thick kind covered in giant sea salt, and as soon as the bags were opened, the car was filled with the sound of munching and chewing instead of the endless nagging. We'd wash it all down with miniature Juicy Juice box drinks Mom and Dad bought in mammoth quantities. By the time we finished, the entire back seat was covered in pretzel crumbs, sea salt and little round balls of puffed rice. Add some solid grape juice stains on our clothes plus the empty juice cartons rattling around at our feet like colorful grenades, and it looked like a battlefield.

I recall one particular trip right around Valentine's Day. I was in 5th grade and my school teacher brought in a ten-pound jar of little candy hearts, the kind that come in a variety of pastel colors with little messages written on them and seem to appear only around Valentine's Day. As a little Valentine's treat, our teacher held a contest. She told us whoever could come closest to guessing the number of hearts in the jar would take the whole thing home. Well, lo and behold, I had the best guess and carted my weighty prize home just in time for our family to go on a long road trip.

Andreya sat in the middle and was the keeper of the candy. There was a constant dipping of hands into the jar as we chewed our way through the ten pounds of chalky hearts, laughing at their silly messages and making up some of our own. As if taking part in a lengthy disappearing magic trick, we polished off the entire jar in just two days, and I ended up with rainbow-colored poop for a week. All these years later, even the sight of those little hearts makes me want to gag. But for that one glorious trip they were like manna straight from the hand of God.

When food wasn't enough to pacify us, my parents would move to step two—slushies! With the discovery of slushies, we found out to our delight that our parents were not above bribery. I really can't recall how the whole slushie craze started, but once it began there was no stopping it. Somewhere in our travels we kids got our hands on some delicious 7 Eleven slushies, and life was never the same again. When we stopped to fill up with gas—and let me tell you our gas-guzzling station wagon had to stop a lot —it was go time.

I had an internal sensor that would begin to beep when we were due for a slushie stop. I knew it was bribery, I knew it was desperation, and I didn't care. We had my parents on the ropes. I'd stare out the window searching intently for that beautiful green 7 Eleven sign. Upon sighting one, I'd holler in delight as my stomach began to gurgle in anticipation. As the boat (our nickname for the car) pulled up to the pump I had one hand on my seat belt buckle and the other on the door handle ready to launch out of the car as quickly as possible. With reckless abandon I ejected, speeding toward the glass doors and the horrified attendants who saw three tiny children hurtling toward them with breakneck speed. Once inside the store, I made a beeline for the slushie-making machine. First come, first served.

Breathing heavily from exertion, I grabbed a small cup and began the sacred art of mixing. I couldn't settle for just a single-flavor slushie. Oh no, that would have been far too simple and anticlimactic. I put in a dab of this and then a dab of that until I had a little of everything. Landon and Dreya were right beside me as we all jostled for position like piglets fighting for a teat. I always saved the best for last: Mountain Dew. Nothing compared to the neon-green, over-caffeinated sludge. It was the drink of the gods. When I placed my hand upon the Mountain Dew lever I entered into a semi-sacred moment. In that instant I believed there was a God and that He was good.

To this day I still get giddy at the thought of a slushie, and whenever the weather begins to turn warm with the coming of spring, I feel the urge to once again return to my roots and make my way to Slushie Mecca.

When the final remnants of slushie had been noisily slurped up, it was time for something else to occupy us. So to amuse ourselves we turned to the tape deck. The food and slushies and games of musical seats were all well and good, but if it had not been for our magical tape player to whisk us away into different worlds, I think we all would have killed each other. We spent countless hours listening to the tales of Adventures in Odyssey, Psalty the Singing Song Book and Hank the Cow Dog. We heard them all at least a half dozen times, and yet somehow they never grew old. They sucked us in, capturing our imaginations, making us tremble and laugh and even shed a few tears on the leather seats. And while we were wrapped up in these parallel realities, my father kept driving and driving and driving.

Sometimes Mom would read aloud to us. Since Dad never let us turn on the air-conditioning because apparently it "used too much gas," we had the windows rolled down to keep from melting to death. It didn't take long for those old leather seats to start heating up, and before you knew it your legs were all sweaty and nasty and would stick to the leather. So Mom would do her best to read over the roar of the engine and the rushing wind as the three of us leaned in as closely as we could.

When Mom grew hoarse, Dad would start telling stories. He'd make them up right there on the spot. Now these weren't your average little kid stories. They would go on for hours and hours and even stretch from one day to the next. He would have us hanging on his every word as he pulled grand stories of adventure and intrigue straight from his bottomless imagination like a modern day bard. We would interrupt him to ask questions about things, and he'd suddenly veer off down a whole new trail to give the story behind the story or elaborate on the shady characters that hung on the fringes of his tales. And all the while, he just kept driving along down the road until we finally arrived at our destination. What awaited us there is a whole other story.

Supporters and Churches

Those long rides in the station wagon always ended somewhere, for good or for bad. Mom and Dad tried their best to describe for us the people we were about to meet and how much they loved all of us. But to me they were just strangers. That's one of the weird things about being an MK. There's this whole network of churches and people who seem to know everything about you and have watched your entire life unfold through the various family newsletters across the years, but you have no clue who any of them really are. Then, in the blink of an eye, when you're standing on their front steps in some unknown town, these folks morph from a name on a mailing list you've seen year after year as you're licking and sticking stamps onto envelopes to flesh and blood people who smell and smile and pinch your cheeks while clucking about how much you've grown.

They invite you in, and for an evening or a day you are treated like long lost family. They stuff you to the gills with all sorts of adult foods and ask you a million questions while Mom and Dad sit silently by, giving you "the look," which basically means "Don't say anything inappropriate." When all is said and done and it's well past your bedtime and you've been bored for hours, you are finally tucked into a strange, creaky bed with old patterned sheets and more frilly, lace-covered pillows than you know what to do with. And after plenty of tossing and turning, sleep arrives.

You awake the next morning to the smell of eggs and bacon and the sound of a foreign alarm clock and it's like Groundhog Day as you prepare to do everything all over again.

The Letter

I was in middle school, and it was a Monday when mom and dad called all of us kids together for an emergency family meeting. They explained that we'd had a significant decline in our monthly support over the past few months. A number of our supporters for one reason or another had decreased their giving, or stopped all together. It was one of those strange moments as a kid where I could tell that my parents were worried. This was not something to be taken lightly, and I felt their anxiety in the pit of my stomach.

The news suddenly made the recent change in our family's diet much clearer. We'd been eating a whole lot of rice and veggies, and what little chicken we used to get had mysteriously disappeared. Most disturbing to me, though, was the fact that the snacks in the pantry had vanished. Previously, when I had complained about the lack of snacks I was pointed to the large stock of home-grown bananas hanging outside the front door and advised I could eat my fill. Apparently the diet change wasn't enough. We were still in big financial trouble with little hope on the horizon for things to change.

I didn't really know what to do with the bad news, but as I walked back to school I found myself praying with each new step. I was afraid that we might have to leave PNG, and I would be forced to go back to that terrible Spring Garden Elementary School I attended when we were last in America. Maybe we would be crammed into another tiny apartment like the one where mom and dad kept trying to pretend that we were just camping because the house we were SUPPOSED to stay in got condemned for water damage and razed the week before we got home on furlough. I could feel the fear seeping in around the edges slowly taking hold of me. Would God take care of us? Would God provide manna like he did all those years ago to Israel?

I was reminded again of our dire financial situation that evening when we sat down to a dinner consisting of baked potatoes. There was not even any cheese to sprinkle on because cheese was too expensive. Baked potatoes without cheese might as well not be baked potatoes as far as I was concerned. This was a new low.

Later that week I picked up the mail on my way home for lunch. As usual, none of the letters were addressed to me. I plopped them down on the table wondering what we were going to eat. We probably couldn't afford peanut butter, so a PB and J was out of the question. That meant I'd be scrounging for leftovers, or there were always those rapidly browning bananas covered in fruit flies hanging just outside the door.

Not having much motivation to check the barren fridge, I randomly opened one of the letters and began to read.

Dear Michael, Bev and Family,

I hope this letter finds you all doing well. It has been a long time since we have been in contact. In fact, if I recall correctly it has been over 10 years. Wow, how time flies. God recently laid your family on my heart and I had a sense that I was supposed to send you some money. Please accept the following check as a gift.

I cautiously unfolded the check tucked into the corner of the envelope. When I saw the amount I almost passed out. The check was for $5,000. I looked at the date on the envelope and felt chills run down my spine. The post mark on the letter was over 6-weeks old, which meant half-way around the world the Holy Spirit had been moving in the heart of a far removed elderly lady before our family was even in need. What I was holding in my hand was modern day manna. I don't know how my parents did it all those years, trusting month after month that God would provide for us. I can only hope someday to have a faith as deep as theirs.

I have a son of my own now, and with another baby on the way I sometimes struggle to trust that God will provide for us on my youth pastor's salary. I have to fight the urge to take matters into my own hands rather than entrust myself into the hands of God, but then in my moments of weakness I often go back to that $5,000 check. I remember again what it was like being a 13-year-old boy opening that precious letter. The same tears of awe well up in my eyes, and I am given strength to believe anew that the God who provided all those years ago will continue to be faithful.

Lost

I might be divulging too many family secrets here, but what kind of a book of memoirs would this be without any really juicy insider stories? When we were home on furlough and driving across the country to visit people, we did not have the luxury of amenities such as a cell phone and a GPS navigation device. I know it's hard to believe, but we had to use these strange, archaic folded paper things called maps. As I say this I realize just how old I sound, which is kind of crazy since I'm only 30. My father, much to his credit, has an amazing geographical memory, but he has an equally impressive stubborn streak. When you put those two traits together you have a recipe for disaster, because when you go overseas for years at a time and then come home, roads and landmarks change. We would often find ourselves driving over Pennsylvania's back roads with Dad looking for a mysterious farmhouse that no longer existed. The more lost we became, the more tense things became in the car, until the tension was so thick I could almost taste its bitter presence on the end of my tongue along with the leftover flavor of my last juice box.

My mother would be up front praying quietly to herself while doing her best to try to find the names of the roads zipping by on the old Atlas map, but map-reading was not really her strong point. After my father finally broke down and admitted he was lost, he would pull over by the side of the road and shut off the engine.

In the silence that followed I could just barely make out my mother's muttered prayers and my father's annoyed exhale as he took the map and scanned it to figure out where in the world we were. We were usually a long way from where we were supposed to be. Yet somehow, by the grace of God, we always made it to our final destination, even if it took two or three times as long as it was supposed to. Perhaps God's answer to my mother's prayers was that this gave us an opportunity to grow in patience. But instead, those tense moments in the car left me with an illogical fear of being lost I still wrestle with today, even with my iPhone in the car.

For some people being lost is an adventure; for me it's complete misery. In fact that's probably an understatement. When I get lost I become angry and irrational. It's as if someone flips a switch and my sanity tumbles out the window like an apple core given the heave ho out of a car doing 70 miles an hour down the highway. In my worst moments I confess I have pounded the steering wheel and yelled angrily at God asking why He let this happen, as if He were the one who managed to take the wrong turn or miss the exit. My fear of being lost stretches farther back that our many car trips on furlough. I can trace the fear all the way back to one perilous day in the Papua New Guinean jungles.

My parents were very close friends of a Finnish/British missionary couple with whom they had gone through orientation. Uncle Alan, as I knew him, was a brilliant linguist and musician. He spoke numerous languages and was the most intellectual and cultured person I knew. His wife, Ritva, was a magnificent piano player and cooked the best cinnamon rolls known to man. Mom would tell us the story of the first night of their three day bush backpacking trip to prepare them for life in PNG. All the new missionaries fresh off the plane were sent into the jungle to make a structure in which to sleep. As they went outside, the heavens opened up, welcoming these brave souls with a tremendous tropical downpour. Now my mom was a lifetime Girl Scout and my father could make or fix just about anything, so the two of them built the best fort you can imagine. From inside their dry shelter, Dad saw poor Uncle Alan standing in the streaming rain, soaked to the bone, with his drooping shoulders and a handful of sticks, completely helpless. He must have been wondering what on earth he was doing in this crazy island a million miles from home. That's the thing about the call of God. It never takes you to the places you expected to go, and yet somewhere along the way you realize you are precisely where you are supposed to be. You struggle forward one day at a time filled with hopes and dreams and questions and fears as you try to allow God to make something beautiful out of your life.

Years later our family went out to visit this couple in

the village where they were translating the Bible. The small JAARS plane landed on a grass airstrip seemingly in the middle of nowhere and dropped us off. From there we had to hike about four hours in to the village. A short way into the hike it became clear that we had people who wanted to go at very different speeds, so we split up into two groups. I started off with the slow group, but soon became tired of their lagging pace. There was only one trail, so I took off from the back group determined to catch the speedsters up front. All by myself, I walked and walked through the dense forest. I knew there was supposed to be a river somewhere up ahead where we were all going to meet and grab lunch. I kept walking for what felt like forever and still no river. Slowly the sounds of the forest began to creep into my consciousness and I became nervous. What if I were lost? Had I strayed from the correct path? I began to panic and could feel my chest tightening like I was having an asthma attack making it hard for me to breathe. With tears streaming down my face and my body taught with fear, I began to run back the way I'd come, shouting for Mom and Dad with terrified intensity. I sprinted as fast as my short legs would take me, but there was nothing except me and the birds chattering in the trees. I envisioned myself starving to death lost in the woods. Finally around a corner the slow group emerged with my dad in the lead. He scooped me up into his strong arms and hushed my cries until they became just a whimper. Everything was okay; I wasn't lost anymore.

After returning to America for college I often felt like that lost little boy again. I traded in the dense jungles of Papua New Guinea for the confusing landscape of American culture, but I was still lost. Only this time I knew that my dad was half-way around the world and could not save me anymore. In fact, nobody was coming to save me. I had to find my new cultural bearings and pull myself together.

I listened to the stories of my fellow MK friends, and at the root of their tales was the same sense of lostness that hung over me like a dense mist. We were all running around trying to find our way, and yet none of us seemed to know what in the world we were doing. The resounding sense was that we were culturally, socially, and spiritually lost. While knowing that others were struggling was in some way reassuring because it meant that my turbulent experience of re-entry was normal, it did not exactly bring me hope that I would soon find my way in this strange American jungle.

Many of my friends went back to PNG within a few years of us graduating in search of closure. They hopped on planes and made the long trek back to our little island world like pilgrims on a spiritual journey. It was as if covering their feet in that rich red clay would somehow provide the miraculous awakening they so desperately longed for, but like many pilgrims all they found waiting for them at their holy destination was dirt and sky and un-met expectations.

The ghosts of days gone bye greeted them at the airstrip, sauntered down familiar roads and stared through the windows of old houses now filled with unknown faces. The barbed wire fence ringing Ukarumpa was a harsh reminder that for Americans like us this was not home. The part words of this sacred shrine were more curse than blessing. Those who dared return were stricken with sadness at the life now gone forever and hopelessness in the face of the jumbled life that loomed ahead.

When I saw the results of my friend's efforts I did not make the journey back to the little blue house on the corner. I figured that a place is never as sacred as the memories we keep of it. I preferred the untarnished falsehoods I had concocted to the painful truth that actually existed. There were no miracles waiting for me, and I was still a little boy lost in the jungle waiting for someone to save me.

The Mystery Chauffeur

I have had my share of seasons where I felt out of touch with God. Seasons where it seemed like my prayers were bouncing off a glass ceiling and going nowhere. In spite go those seasons of silence and spiritual drought I still believe strongly that our God is Immanuel, which means "God is with us." There have been too many instances where I have seen God show up in incredible ways. The collective result of these experiences is a deep rooted confidence that God is faithful even when all seems lost.

The most radical of these crazy God experiences took place in 5th grade when our family flew into a small airport in the U.S while home on furlough. It was the sort of airport that actually made me feel like I was back overseas. Rustic and sparse, the place had seen better and busier days. Even our plane was well passed its prime with worn seat covers and rickety tray tables.

I think our family's luggage made up the majority of pieces spewed forth onto the baggage carousel. Dragging all of our suitcases with us on wobbly wheels, we made our way outside where someone was supposed to be waiting to drive us the hour and a half to our next destination. We did not know who exactly would be picking us up, but we assumed that the missionary family at the tiny airport in the middle of nowhere would be easy to spot. We set up camp on the curbside. Standing at attention, we made eye contact with the few strangers milling about wondering which of them was our mystery chauffeur. The answer was, none of them.

Everyone else from our flight was long gone, and as the minutes went by, soon only my father was standing, looking, hoping that somebody was coming for us. My mother sat with us kids, but I could hear her praying quietly for someone to come. An hour went by and then another. Still we waited. We had no name, no phone number, no way to get in touch with anyone to help.

We sat in the hazy dusk watching the occasional plane drift in like an unexpected guest, and then the last rim of the sun disappeared and darkness was upon us. Hungry bellies were rumbling and patience was wearing thin as we pulled out sweatshirts and jackets to thwart the chill of the night. The hanging lights in front of the waiting area slowly hummed to life, and we were stranded beneath their dim luminescence.

There was the sound of a sputtering engine and then out of the darkness pulled up a large van. The car shut off and out stepped a kind looking man. I watched and listened from my suitcase seat as he approached my father.

I stood up and stretched my legs. I was more than ready to be out of this dingy place. At least the van would have heat. Dad walked over to us.
"This gentleman is not who we've been waiting for." My heart dropped and I slumped back onto the suitcase. Beside me, I thought my brother was going to start crying.

Dad carried on, "He does, however, happen to be going to the same place we are, and he has offered us a ride."
Being a kid, I didn't think twice about the unusualness of this occurrence. Apparently my parents hadn't watched enough horror movies to question whether or not being picked up by a complete stranger in a large van at an airport in the middle of nowhere was a good idea, but next thing I knew, our family was cruising down the highway in the van.

Our mystery chauffeur dropped us off at the address my dad provided him. We piled out of the van, unloaded the luggage from the back and turned to get a look at where we would be staying. It was late, and we were hoping somebody would still be up. Mom and dad did a quick check to make sure we had everything. We turned around to thank the man and could barely believe our eyes.

The man and the van were gone. They had vanished into thin air.

I will go to my grave swearing that God sent an angel that night to pick us up, because that's the kind of God we serve--the God who hears a mother's prayers and sends an angel in a van to pick up a stranded missionary family.

Chapter 4
America, Home Sweet Home?

"It doesn't matter how many times you leave, it will always hurt to come back and remember what you once had and who you once were. Then it will hurt just as much to leave again, and so it goes over and over again. Once you've started to leave, you will run your whole life."

- Charlotte Eriksson

The Unspoken Reality

Missionary kids are a strange breed. If you've ever hung out with them you know what I mean. I often joke that I can spot a missionary or an MK a hundred yards away. They just have a certain aura about them. When I finally get around to telling people I grew up overseas, the greatest compliment they can pay me is to tell me they had no idea I was an MK. Those are the moments when I know I've really adapted and I'm not putting out the all-too-common creepy, maladjusted MK vibe.

Always having to move and make new friends knowing you'll only be in a place for a couple of years takes its toll on you. Missionary kids generally respond to the struggle in two different ways. The outgoing MKs, like me, see it as a challenge to make as many new friends and do as many new things as possible. Kids of this type tend to do well wherever you put them, and they don't have too much trouble adjusting. They squeeze the most life out of every experience. Now the bad part about MKs with this mindset is that when they have to go, it really sucks, because they leave all of their new friends and places behind, and they know realistically they will probably never see or hear from them again. Out of sight, out of mind—that's just the way it is. Long-distance friendships don't really work most of the time.

Then there is the other type of MKs who intentionally choose not to make a lot of new friends because they know how difficult it will be to say good-bye. After leaving enough people behind, they just can't handle any more relational pain. My sister is a perfect example of this type. So for MKs like her, traveling and moving to new places is terrible. She would spend our whole furlough being miserable, longing to go back to PNG to her old friends and the life she knew.

Both types of MKs share something in common, something I experienced firsthand my senior year in PNG. My two best friends were juniors. Knowing I'd be returning to the United States after graduation, they began to pull away about midway through my senior year. Nothing was ever said; it just sort of happened. They started moving on with their lives as if I'd basically disappeared. Previously, I'd always been the one doing the leaving. It was strange to be on the receiving end for once.

So there I was with about six months to go, and I pretty much lost my best friends. I thought we were going to be friends for life. I assumed they would one day be the groomsmen at my wedding. And then, bam! Without a word, I was on the outside looking in. It was awful, and yet I don't know if they realized what they were doing. After all our years of friendship together, it crushed my spirit to watch the relationships suffer a slow, bitter death.

People often think being a missionary kid is a constantly amazing experience, because that's all they ever hear. We MKs selectively tell people our "cool" stories. We share about a mysterious and magical world, unlike anything they've ever experienced, because we so desperately want to be liked and accepted. We want to be funny and interesting, and this is our best shot. But while we're clambering to impress, we fail to tell listeners the whole story. We keep the bad parts to ourselves. We don't talk about lost relationships and broken dreams and always feeling out of place. We don't share the stories of sadness and confusion and isolation, because nobody really wants to hear those. So in reality, we lie. We lie to others and to ourselves. We envision a perfect world that never existed and this makes our current life seem drab and miserable by comparison. We move from place to place and people group to people group, always looking to start over as we try to find the unreachable perfection we are pursuing.

After years of this pursuit I finally woke up and saw my past for what it was. I felt guilty for having negative thoughts about PNG and the people I'd grown up among. I felt like I should just let go of the bad and hold on to the good, but that's not reality. The reality is this: growing up as an MK was both wonderful and terrible all at the same time. I wouldn't trade my childhood for anything, but for the sake of my own sanity I needed to be honest.

Hugs

Growing up in PNG I was taught not to hug girls, certainly not to hold girls' hands, and God forbid I should kiss a girl before we were married. Follow those three rules, and I would be safe. While part of this conservatism arose out of the Christian world in which I lived, part of it was culturally conditioned. In PNG men and women spend most of their time apart. Men hang out with men and women hang out with women. It is very common to see men walking around holding hands, not as a sign of sexual interest, but as an act of friendship. It would always crack me up when I'd see a string of guys walking down the road all linked together holding pinkies like some sort of human chain.

While women's breasts were not considered to be sexual, women's thighs were. It's not terribly difficult to figure out the reasoning behind this, so you can imagine that scooping somebody up in a big old hug and holding them close was deemed to be a very sexual maneuver. I just sort of went through life with the mindset of associating hugs with sex.

I arrived at college for freshman orientation at the ripe old age of 17, ready to take on America. To my sheer amazement I watched as people gave out hugs left and right. What was going on here?! Had I unknowingly committed to attend a school the equivalent of a modern day Sodom and Gomorrah?

To make matters worse, all these girls I didn't know were trying to give me hugs as well! They were trying to suck me into their wayward ways. Lord, save me, I cried out. I didn't know what to do. So I awkwardly did my best to attempt the Christian side hug thing, waiting for the stripper poles to come down out of the sky at any moment and the women to start flinging off their clothes. These people were all a bunch of crazy Southern swingers.

By the end of freshman orientation I'd been hugged more times by more girls than in my entire life. I was pretty sure I'd lost my virginity in the midst of a few bodacious hugs and was, by the look of things, piling up some serious time in purgatory as penalty for my deviant hugging extravaganza.

What baffled me was that nobody else seemed bothered by the hedonism taking place. I mean these folks were in my Bible classes, went to church and talked about Jesus and then—BOOM—a big hugging frenzy. I'd heard for years that America was going to hell in a hand-basket, but now I knew firsthand it was true. They were tumbling down the slippery slope of promiscuity as fast as they possibly could. They were hugging their way to perdition at such a sickening pace that the angels must surely be in tears.

When the kid with the "free hugs" T-shirt appeared I thought the end times were about to rain down on us. Here before my very eyes was a hug prostitute with arms wide open for one and all. I wanted to run away. I did not belong in this God-forsaken place. I wanted to print a shirt proclaiming, "No hugs. Not now. Not ever." Instead, I awkwardly absorbed the fewest hugs possible while praying for forgiveness.

When I finally divulged my feelings and fears about all the hugging to a friend he burst into a hysterical fit of laughter! But I didn't understand. Premarital sex was not a laughing matter. This was serious. We needed some boundaries in this place. Perhaps even revival.

When he finally stopped laughing, my friend explained to me the error of my ways. Here, *in America*, he explained (emphasizing this point very clearly for me), *there is nothing sexual about hugs.* You cannot imagine the incredible sense of relief I felt when I heard this.

But along with the relief there was the inevitable companion of foolishness. Once again I was the outsider. After all, it was me who was the strange one, not all of the sweet tea–drinking Southerners. I wondered if I would ever fit in. Would I ever understand all the little unspoken cultural nuances of this new world in which I lived or would I always feel awkward? I never became a hugger. I guess 17 years of not hugging had an effect on me, but I did learn to master the side hug and to not judge people based on their hugging. I've also learned a few other things here and there. Cultural adaptation is a slow process, and progress often comes at the hands of humiliation; but like a chameleon, I've learned to blend in.

The Windjammer

The small, six-seater plane circled the short landing strip. I tugged on Dad's shirt and pretty much had to yell to get his attention over the whining of the twin engines.

"What are all those ponds doing around the airstrip?" I asked. I figured my dad knew everything, and in this case he did.

"They're from World War II when the Japanese bombed the Allied forces stationed here."

I sat back in my seat. "Cool!" Apparently nobody bothered to fill in the huge holes, and over time they'd filled up with water. As we swooped down for our final descent I could see that most of them were completely covered over with dark green algae. Just like the bomb craters, not much had changed in the small town of Wewak since the war. Most things had just grown a little older and become a little more worn down.

My dad was responsible for all the Wycliffe missionaries in this area of the country, so our whole family flew out twice a year to join him while he worked with the different Bible translators. We usually flew out during the school holidays and stayed at the comfy SIL guesthouse for about two weeks. Wewak was on the Southern coast of Papua New Guinea and was hot all the time; it was the kind of heat that saps the energy right out of you as soon as you step outside.

When all of us kids were tired of watching the three fuzzy channels on TV and couldn't bear to play another game of war or double solitaire, my mom would read to us. We must have spent a couple hundred hours all lying underneath the fan wishing it would go faster as we listened to her. Those were some of the best times as we slipped into strange literary worlds and for a while forgot about everything else going on around us. But eventually even Mother's reading ran its course and tension began to build when our cooped-up energy mixed with the sweaty heat took its toll. Before there was a mutiny my mother would adeptly offer us a diversion. Handing us a couple kina, the local currency, she told us to go buy ice cream. Those words were like music to our ears.

We'd all run out of the house and down the hill to the little convenience store with its magical case of frozen ice cream bars. There was a variety of colorful options, but we all knew there was really only one legitimate choice: The Golden Gay Time. No, I'm not making the name up. They were the most delicious ice cream bars you can imagine. As soon as you took one out of the freezer, it was a race against the sweltering heat. You had a little under two minutes to eat the entire thing, or it melted and slowly slid off the wooden popsicle stick. It was a furious frozen eating competition, and I never lost. Long before I was back at the top of the hill, all that remained was a dry stick. When it came to Golden Gay Times, there was no messing around.

On the days when we didn't loiter around the guesthouse, we went to the beach. There were a couple different spots we would frequent. One was a waveless black sand beach that looked like it came straight out of a National Geographic magazine. About 15 feet into the water was a sprawling coral reef filled with spotted and striped fish of every size, color and shape. Scooting in and out amongst the underwater plant life and giant heads of coral was a never-ending parade of magnificent creatures. Starfish and spiky sea urchins were tucked into nooks and crannies, and we'd troll the ocean floor for sand dollars to take home. Out along the edges of the reef where it seemed like the sea floor dropped off into oblivion, the water turned into a rich dark blue and grew markedly cooler.

I was always nervous when I hit the deep waters. There was something scary about staring down through my snorkel goggles into the seemingly bottomless blue fathoms. In spite of my fear, I couldn't help but venture out to the edge to spy on the much larger fish lurking there and the occasional shark circling far below. Swimming on the coral outskirts I had one of my most amazing life experiences.

Minding my own business, I was flippering away when I accidentally drifted into a massive swirling school of fish. One moment everything was clear blue water; then suddenly all I could see were tiny silver fish swimming all around me. I tried to reach out and touch them but they mysteriously eluded me, always staying a fraction out of reach as I swam about in their midst, lost in a world of shimmering metallic scales. While treading water, the fish were moving around me like one giant organism that had somehow swallowed me into its bowels. I hung suspended in the water, watching in amazement as the fish dipped and darted.

When they didn't seem to be going anywhere, I decided to see how big the school really was, and I struck out swimming. Stroke after stroke I tried to escape the school, only to find myself still surrounded by this enormous mass of fish. There were hundreds of thousands of them, all swimming together for survival in a flowing choreographed dance.

After what seemed like an immensely long time, I finally came to the school's edge. From my new vantage point I stared at the school of glimmering fish as they were blown backward and forward by the underwater currents rippling them like an enormous field of wheat in the wind. It was breathtakingly beautiful, a truly sacred moment.

As much as the black sand beach was peaceful and filled with an unending world of underwater mysteries, it was not my favorite beach location. That was reserved for the Windjammer, an old rundown restaurant right on the beach, whose wooden exterior had been carved to look like an enormous crocodile. The chefs had a scant menu, most of which was not available half the time since they were always out of basic food items, so we usually ended up ordering chips with tomato sauce. Let me translate this meal into American for you: French fries and ketchup! I was sorely surprised when I came back to the States and ordered a hamburger with chips only to be served a small handful of Lays Potato Chips to go along with my burger. I made that mistake only once. While chips and tomato sauce were a rare treat for us, it wasn't the food that made the Windjammer so special: it was the waves.

It was a windy day in the middle of storm season and seas were rough. The walls of the Windjammer shuddered and surging white-capped waves crashed into the shore, pounding the beach with mighty blows. Landon and I watched the eight-foot waves, licking sea salt from our lips in anticipation. Two scrawny warriors, we waded into the fray and fought our way through the mammoths that kept rolling in one after another. We were at the mercy of the churning waves as they dashed us all about, throwing us head-over-heels in wild somersaults and barrel roles. My mother sat on the beach like our high priestess praying fervently as she watched the battle unfolding.

In the distance black storm clouds loomed threateningly, but I was not to be denied my ride. Seeing the perfect wave approaching, I paddled like crazy to get out in front of its watery girth trying to catch the top of its crest before it broke over me with the might of an enraged battle stallion. There was that singularly glorious moment as I felt my body get caught up in the power of the wave, and I knew what was about to happen. The wave engulfed my world and everything was rushing water and blackness as I closed my eyes tight. I stiffened my body, thrusting my arms out in front me using my hands as a wedge to cut through the water and, as the wave shot me forward, a tiny human arrow launched from the heart of the sea.

The wave was a wild stallion bucking and braying as I held on for dear life. At last tamed, it gently nudged me onto the shore. Sputtering as I gasped for breath, I crawled to my feet. The battle was won. I roared victoriously and ran full tilt back toward the battlefield to do it all over again. By the end of the day I'd been dragged along the ocean floor so many times that my legs and chest were raw. I'd been punched and pounded purple by the waves, but time and time again I emerged victorious until the high priestess called me home from the battlefield. I would live to fight another day.

My freshman year of college, all of my friends talked about going to the beach over Spring Break. With the black sand beach and the Windjammer in mind I was so excited to go! I couldn't believe what I saw when we arrived at the ocean: there were crowds of people sprawled out all across the beach. In Wewak we always had the place to ourselves. When I got over that shock I quickly realized there were no waves. There must be a coral reef, I thought to myself. But I almost didn't make it past the first tiny wave that ran up and over my feet; the water was freezing! Why did all these people in the water look so happy? I toughed it out, wanting to see what sort of fish they had here. I put my head under water and could hardly believe my eyes. Everything was so sandy and murky I could barely see my own hands under water. I went farther and farther out hoping to find the reef and all the fish I just assumed were there. Finally I went back to shore. No waves and no reef. This beach sucked. All my friends wanted to do anyway was lay out and get a tan. Heck, I could do that anywhere there was sunshine without getting covered in sticky sand. I lay there with them bored and annoyed. They had no idea what they were missing.

ID Please

Turning 16 and applying for your learner's permit to start driving is part of classic American upbringing. It's a rite of passage into the impending world of adulthood, and a sleep-stealing, horrifying step for parents when they release control and hand over the car keys. It's the fear-inducing experience that starts with trying to dodge cones and cars in a big parking lot, and after a whole lot of calling on the name of Jesus (some good and some bad), tears and shouting, eventually leads to the inevitable call of the open road. Learning to drive is a symbol of freedom and responsibility. It is a badge of honor earned through the mastery of the ancient art of parallel parking. The whole experience gives new meaning to the verse challenging us to work out our faith with fear and trembling, as both driver and parent sit in the car in reversed positions for the first time—both praying, both scared, both unsure of what is about to take place.

In PNG I also learned how to drive, but not in typical American fashion. To begin with, I had to drive on the opposite side of the road. I guess I can thank the British Empire and the blessed Queen for that. I never drove much above 30 miles an hour because the roads were so bad. I'm not sure who to blame more for that one—God for sending ridiculous amounts of rain or the PNG prime minister, who never spent any money on road upkeep. I spent most of my time trying to avoid the holy trinity of Ps—pedestrians, potholes and pigs. Oh, and did I mention there was only one traffic light in the entire country? None of those things prepared me particularly well for American highways.

When I came back to the States for college, my international license didn't transfer, and I basically had to learn all over again how to drive, which meant I was in college and didn't have a license or any sort of government-issued photo ID. I know this seems crazy, but you would be amazed how many things there are for which you need a photo ID. For example, when I'd go to an R-rated movie with a bunch of my college friends I would always be asked for my photo ID because I looked like I was 15. It would make me so embarrassed because I would have to try to explain my situation while all my friends stood by and watched. I'd hand over my college ID and the ticket sales person would carefully examine it to see if it was a fake before hesitantly shooing me in.

Other times I'd go up to the ticket counter, and when the ticket agents asked for ID I'd hand them my passport. That always threw them off. There would be this awkward pause as they stared at the passport sitting in front of them not sure exactly what to do, as if I were trying to play some sort of a practical joke. In the rural South where I attended college, people didn't exactly go around brandishing passports. Most folks had probably never left the state, let alone thought about getting a passport to leave the country.

Flying continentally without a traditional photo ID was the worst. They'd look at me and see a young man with no driver's license who was born in some weird country called Papua New Guinea. And when they opened my passport and found it had stamps from all over the world including places like India, Cambodia and Egypt, those airport security guards suddenly turned really serious. Without fail, I would get "random" searched every time I flew. It didn't matter where I was going, I was somehow magically selected. No driver's license = automatic search! They would look through all my stuff and give me the good old pat down as if I were the next Osama Bin Laden waiting to board their tiny plane flying out of the highly illustrious city of Greenville, South Carolina, which nobody in the world has ever heard of. I mean really, people? Is Greenville to Lancaster on a little plane with about 50 people a prime target for terrorists? Based on my experience, it was clear they were taking no chances.

I started wearing a suit every time I flew to see if it made any difference. It didn't, but at least I felt better about myself. After they had solidified that I was not a threat to national security without ever cracking a smile or being friendly, in spite of my attempts to be cordial, they allowed me to board my plane and be on my way just like the rest of my fellow Americans.

It's weird, but I didn't feel like I was a "real" American until I finally held my driver's license in my hands. Until then I was still an outsider bumming rides everywhere, always at the mercy of those around me. I was the backward MK who still didn't get it. Others may not have viewed me this way, but it was my perception. It was just one more example of how I was different, another way to prove I wasn't from around these parts and still had a lot to learn. I hated this feeling, and when I finally had a driver's license to put in my wallet and I could leave my passport safely at home, I felt like a million bucks.

A Pack of Stray Dogs

I realized quickly that in America people take pet ownership very seriously. Dogs and cats become members of the family, and their passing is often marked with deep sadness and even a burial ceremony. While I was in seminary I was asked on multiple occasions whether or not we would be reunited with our pets in heaven. For pet owners this is not a laughing matter. I think some folks would rather see their dog waiting for them at the pearly gates than a few of their own family members, but I won't get into that.

In Africa you don't find people walking their dogs. You certainly don't see folks following dogs around with little plastic gloves to clean up after them. Walkers beware! In a world where families struggle to put food on the table twice a day, there is little room for pampered pets. The dogs live outside and are left to fend for themselves, living off whatever scraps they can scrounge up after meals and in the trash. Most of them are skinny little mutts with brown saggy skin scarred from too many tussles over stray bites of food. Packs of these wild dogs roamed the beaches in Senegal struggling to survive.

I was busy digging in the sand out in front of our house with my blue plastic shovel when danger showed up. A pack of mangy dogs came up from the beach looking for a little morsel of white meat for dinner. They began to close in around me with their ribs sticking out in all directions and their yellow teeth dripping saliva, ready to bite. Unable to defend myself with my bucket and shovel I began to scream. Fido, Fifi, Fluffy and the rest sensed they were about to feast.

Suddenly the old Senegalese man who guarded our house appeared. He was always so stoic and regal wearing traditional African dress and an embroidered hat. I'd never seen him run before, but there he was, sprinting at the snarling dogs, shouting at the top of his lungs and hurling stones in their direction. They were no match for his fury, and skittered away with their tails between their legs. He picked me up and wiped away my tiny tears, speaking soothingly to me in French. Everything was going to be okay. I did not know it, but he had just saved my life.

I am still scared to death of dogs—big dogs little dogs, if it has teeth and barks I'm probably afraid of it. My wife keeps asking if we can get a dog. She wonders why I don't jump at the idea of having a little four-legged friend running around the house needing to be fed, watered, walked, bathed, house-trained and taken to the vet. Where do I start? How do I explain that in my world pets aren't even on the radar?

Cyrus the Great

Cyrus was an outdoor cat and one of the few pets we had while we were growing up. Tough as nails, he was a fighter. The scrawny little PNG mutts roaming around scavenging for food and pooping wherever they darn well pleased had it in for Cyrus. With their ribs on clear display and their tiny teeth barred, they would often try to attack Cyrus, but he was a battle-hardened veteran with the scars to prove it. Fearless, he'd sit there with his claws out and stare down the opposition. The foolish dogs that dared to attack inevitably retreated with their tails between their legs and a fresh scratch or two across the nose. For years Cyrus lived outside, pretty much minding his own business except for his occasional attempts to sneak into the house if we left the front door open.

One year our family went away for Christmas, so we asked our PNG neighbors to take care of Cyrus for us. They happily agreed, and we went on our merry way. Upon our return, Dad strolled over to go bring Cyrus back while the rest of us started hauling in our bags from the car. We were standing in the living room when Dad walked back in and immediately called a family meeting. That was never a good sign.

Dad cleared his throat. "Okay...so I'm not sure how exactly to say this, but Cyrus is gone."

I was highly allergic to Cyrus, so I wasn't terribly disturbed by this news, but my brother and sister were mortified. My sister broke into tears. Through sobs she asked every parent's favorite question... "Why?"

"Well, he's dead."

Cue more tears and then another "Why?"

This is probably where my father should have told us a story, but I guess the truth was just too good to withhold.

"Our neighbors ate him for Christmas dinner." There was a long silence as the news sank in. Dad tried his hardest to keep a straight face, but the corners of his mouth keep curling up at the edges, threatening to break out into a smile.

When he'd gone next door and asked about bringing Cyrus back, there was a lot of awkward foot shuffling and looking at the ground. Eventually it came out that he'd been eaten. Apparently there had been a little misunderstanding about the concept of "taking care of" the cat. I mean you can't really blame our neighbors. They couldn't afford much meat and Cyrus was a fat cat. He probably fed the whole family. That's just not the sort of offer you can pass up. I can imagine him sitting as the centerpiece of their Christmas dinner, served with a side of sweet potatoes and an assortment of greens.

We never had another cat after Cyrus. The entire thing was a little too scarring. All those years of scrappy street fighting and staying alive only to wind up as Christmas dinner for our next-door neighbors. Sometimes life just has a strange sense of humor.

The Zoo

I have embraced the fact that I will never be fully adjusted, whatever that phrase is supposed to mean. With each new season of life I find new ways that my upbringing sets me apart from the American culture I now live in. I realize there will never be a day when those differences just fade away. Most assuredly they have diminished over time, but they are always there lurking under the surface.

I noticed this most recently when my son Samuel was born. He is a chubby little guy with a noggin so large we nicknamed him "bison head." He looks like a bobblehead doll, and when he starts teetering over there's no stopping him. When people say he looks like me I try not to be offended.

I find it difficult to make sense of the American paranoia with safety. You have to buy the most up-to-date this and the most up-to-date that. Make people sanitize their hands before they touch your baby. No sleeping on your stomach. The list goes on. It's rather overwhelming, and a far cry from the hand sanitizer free world of PNG where mothers place their babies in large string bags and hang them from the trees to rock to sleep.

I recently heard a story about an American doctor who was forced to prescribe dirt pills for two young boys because their mother was so obsessive about keeping them clean that she practically followed them around with Lysol wipes. What?! I can only imagine trying to explain to my international friends why on earth parents were paying money so their kids could consume dirt. They would think Americans had lost their minds. Upon the conclusion of the story I had to resist the urge to go roll Samuel in dirt, dunk him in the nearest mud puddle and make him share a lollipop with the next-door neighbor's kid. Kids are supposed to get dirty and scrape their knees. If they don't get themselves into at least a few sticky situations, they'll never have any good stories to tell.

Let me begin my next story with a slight tangent. It will all make sense in a minute. I was always short for my age. In fact, I was so short I never even made it onto the national growth chart until middle school when I managed to break into the one percentile. Yes, now only 99% of boys my age were taller than me. I was moving up in the world. My overly excited mother then proceeded to bake me a cake in celebration of my ground-breaking achievement. Perhaps a little more American hormone-riddled meat would have helped speed things along. Apparently our diet of rice, giant Swiss cheese wheels and vegetables was not conducive to bone growth.

Long before I ever made it into the illustrious 1% I was trundling along, looking rather malnourished, holding my father's hand as we walked through the monkey section of the Senegalese zoo. Pink-bottomed baboons and tree monkeys stared at me, too tired to move underneath the blazing midday sun. On the ground near the front of his dusty cage sat an exceptionally large, tan gangly monkey. Wanting to get a closer look at his leathery face and sleepy eyes, I let go of Dad's hand and sauntered over to him. Ducking under the wooden guardrail, I sidled up next to his cage.

Like a flash, his long, hairy arms darted through a sizable hole in the wire mesh cage and he grabbed hold of my leg. With his strong hands clamped around my ankle, he started to pull me toward him. His claws were digging into my skin, and he began to make strangely human sounds of anticipatory delight as he dragged me toward the cage. His lips were peeled back revealing two rows of thick, brown teeth that needed a good tooth brushing. I froze in fear, too terrified to utter so much as a peep. There was nothing I could do to get away from those gnashing teeth.

Standing next to me my shocked father threw down the folder filled with important legal documents we'd just received from the American Embassy and grabbed my other leg with both hands. He and the monkey heaved back and forth in a heated tug-of-war. The monkey was hungry and I looked rather delicious, but my dad wasn't about to have to explain to my mother why her son's leg became a snack.

Finally, the fat ape released me, howling in anger as I escaped his clutches. Dad and I both toppled to the ground and took a moment to catch our breath. My leg was covered in bloody scratch marks, proof of the strange encounter we'd just been through. Very few people can say they've been attacked by a monkey, and I'm willing to bet that even fewer can say it happened in a zoo. Growing up should be dirty and dangerous, at least that's my MK perspective.

Chapter 5
My Spiritual Journey

My spiritual journey has been shaped by the many diverse expressions of the body of Christ; by people past and present from every corner of the globe. Their love and their stories have challenged and inspired me to keep walking with Jesus so that people from every tongue and tribe and nation might know that Jesus is Lord.

The Rubber Tree

If I were to tell you Papua New Guinea is a tropical island in the South Pacific and asked you to picture what types of trees grow there, you would probably picture a coconut tree, or a banana tree or maybe even a mango tree. But if you were to ask me what type of tree I think of when I envision Papua New Guinea, I imagine a rubber tree. You might ask, "What the heck is a rubber tree?" Well, that is not a simple answer. A rubber tree is so many different things to a young boy.

At the base of our yard sat one of the biggest rubber trees for miles around. We would cut little slits in its trunk so the sap would ooze out and harden. Once it dried, the sap was just like rubber. We'd pick off the strips and globs of sap and roll them up to make a small, all-natural bouncy ball. Hence the tree's name: "Bouncy."

The tree is also nature's perfect jungle gym. Rubber trees are a giant maze of bendable branches shooting off in every direction. There is no end to the number of routes a kid can take while climbing about. The long, low-hanging branches function as elevators. I would dangle from a branch as if I were hanging on the monkey bars, and then I would swing out farther and farther toward the end of the branch as it dipped lower and lower until I was standing on the ground. Once there, I would jump upward, still holding on, and the branch would shoot back up carrying me with it as if I were attached to a catapult. Gravity would drag me back down, and as soon as my feet touched the grass I'd launch myself skyward again and again until my arms grew too tired to hold on to the branch, and then I'd let go and lie there in the soft, shaded grass.

The tree was so big that we invented a game called "tree tag." The person who was "it" would have to start on the ground while the rest of us clambered up to our favorite spots. The rubber tree had two thick trunks that split near the bottom, but you could switch from one trunk to the next if you climbed over to the right set of branches. Although an acquired skill learned as a result of a lot of scrapes and sore hands, you could slide down about a ten-foot section of the skinnier trunk like down a fire pole when you needed to escape. We spent a lot of time chasing each other around in that tree and on more than one occasion nearly killed ourselves falling.

When we weren't playing tag on it, the rubber tree was the perfect place to spy on unsuspecting pedestrians. Nestled in the upper branches with a friend or two, we'd sit and watch people walk by on the road below completely unaware as we listened to their conversations. Other times I'd go up there to think and pray. It was a safe haven, and when the wind blew gently on my face and rustled the leaves it sometimes felt like the Holy Spirit was right there beside me in the tree.

To this day my brother and I talk about climbing trees with a religious fervor. We spent a lot of our childhood up in trees. We all have our sacred spaces in life, and for me, that old rubber tree was holy ground. How I long to go back there and climb my way back up to the highest branches and feel the cool breeze against my cheeks and listen as my prayers drift off into the misty mountain morning. It's been over 10 years now since I came back to the US, and I am still searching for my American rubber tree.

Church

Sunday meant church. My parents worked with Wycliffe Bible Translators, a non-denominational missions organization. Why is this important to understand? Well, because it meant that I didn't grow up attending a traditional church. I was never a part of a denomination. I wasn't Presbyterian or Methodist or Pentecostal. It wasn't until I went off to college that I really even began to think about the idea of denominations. To me there were two types of churchgoers: those who went to the early morning service where we lived and those who attended the later service. As far as I was concerned that's as complicated as church needed to be.

I knew my mother was a good Calvinist Presbyterian and my dad, well...he had sort of jumped around. But I didn't have any real sense of denominational affiliation. I hear hip Christians today talking proudly about being post-denominational and I laugh, because there we were, in the middle of the Pacific Ocean, apparently on the cutting edge of Christianity and its move away from denominationalism.

Our family attended the first service. We went to church rain or shine, and had there ever been snow I'm sure we still would have gone. The service was held in the native language of Melanesian Pidgin and was led by the national people who worked alongside the missionaries. I learned how to worship under their humble leadership.

They were people of exuberant praise, singing boisterously along with their ringing electric guitars that always seemed to find a way back to a reggae beat no matter what they sang. They taught me worship is not a performance, it is about a heart longing for God. And when the music ended and the little old lady who sat in the front left pew stopped holding out her final, high-pitched note, which was never in key the rest of us were singing, the people prayed. Oh Lord, how they prayed. They were a people of prayer, a people who believed in the power and presence of the Holy Spirit. They lay on hands and commissioned and blessed and interceded on behalf of the weary and the oppressed. They prayed for revival, straining and laboring in prayer as a community for their own people. Yes, they were warriors in the spiritual realm. Their worship was sweet incense drifting up to heaven, shaking the dominion of darkness. I believe with all my heart that the devil fled and quaked when the PNG people began to sing and pray in the name of Jesus. It wasn't fancy. It wasn't high church or low church. It wasn't steeped in history and theology. It was steeped in real life, steeped in hardship, steeped in the belief that God is present with His people and that He is still Immanuel, steeped in love for one another and for the world. And all those things made it so beautiful.

Of course I didn't always feel this way about the Pidgin church. When I had to get up out of bed early or when I couldn't understand what was being said because the people up front were speaking so fast in a language that wasn't my native tongue that I had no clue what they were saying, I was rather less appreciative. It's more often when I look back that I see the different ways attending the Pidgin service week in and week out shaped my understanding of God and Christianity.

I will be forever indebted to those men and women who week in and week out greeted me with love, lifted their hands without shame and refused to "play" church. This was not some fancy Western game they were now playing to curry favor from the white missionaries who had come over and introduced it to them. This was not just a part of the weekly ritual they endured for the sake of social status. Some of the people had to walk miles to get to church. They came with hearts hungry for God. Sunday was a celebration of a living God, not a monument to a dead religion.

When I returned to the United States for college I spent my entire freshman year church-hopping with friends. I was sorely disappointed and disoriented by what I found. American churches seemed so stiff and impersonal and it felt like, come hell or high water, they were going to make it through the order of service printed in the bulletin in a timely fashion. It didn't help that I was very confused with all the sitting down and standing up and speaking out loud together as a congregation. All the hymns were new to me and seemed to be in a key I could never comfortably sing. I couldn't even enjoy the worship because I switched octaves continually, trying to read all the tiny words for the first time and trying to make sense of what I was singing. I walked away with the impression that church was mostly a social formality.

I was searching for authenticity and openness to the Holy Spirit, but those characteristics were nowhere to be found in the churches I attended. I wanted to be with people to celebrate the victory of Jesus Christ over the powers of darkness and to join hands in spiritual battle, but none of that language ever appeared. There was no talk of demons or angels or spiritual gifts like speaking in tongues or prophecy. To be honest, folks rarely even talked about heaven or hell and the poor Holy Spirit seemed like the "forgotten redheaded stepchild" of the Trinity. There was no real talk about our call to suffer for the sake of Christ. All of these things had defined my experience of church, so when they were stripped away I felt completely out of place.

I missed seeing the faces of people from all around the world worshipping beside me. I missed them dancing, raising their hands and praying in multiple languages. I even missed the twangy, out-of-tune guitars and the off-beat drummers. Yes, my mind was fed, but my heart felt like it was withering. My soul was parched and thirsty for living water. I wanted more than one hour of Christian moralism or a pleasant pep talk and a musical performance with fancy musicians on stage. I got to the point where I didn't even want to go to church anymore. I just went because I felt like it was the right thing to do.

My search for a place to worship led me to a most unexpected place: the Erskine College Gospel Choir. I had no idea what I was getting myself into the first night I showed up. I walked into the Sunday night rehearsal and there were about 70 people standing on risers. There was a wonderful mixture of black and white students, and I felt right at home in the multiracial community. I had never really heard gospel music before, so when the choir director started tearing up the keyboard and then unleashed a rumbling belt so big it filled up the room, I couldn't contain my excitement. The free flowing nature of the music pulled me in and made we want to shout "HALLELUJAH!" at the top of my lungs. This was what I had been looking for.

The next two hours of music were the most profound religious experience I'd had since returning to America. There was no bulletin, no agenda and no intellectualism, only pure and beautiful worship. Just when you thought your body couldn't possibly contain any more high notes and any more passion, the music kept flowing, song after song, coming from somewhere deep within. It was like a river of joy continually washing over us.

On the final song one of the girls stood up and sang a solo. Never in all my life have I heard such a voice. She soared into the stratosphere hitting notes I didn't know were possible after growing up listening to Amy Grant. Every word dripped with emotion. There was a yearning and a desire that could not be contained. We all had tears in our eyes as Nikki unleashed a torrent of praise that brought Jesus down into the room with us. As the final note drifted away into the warm South Carolina night, it left in its wake a sacred silence.

Those two hours each week became my sanctuary from the craziness of life. While I never could get down the whole "clap, sing and sway all at the same time" thing, it didn't matter. As I learned a whole new repertoire of songs outside of the Chris Tomlin and Matt Redman contemporary Christian classics I'd grown up with, I was opened up to a new, vibrant tradition of worship and spirituality so different and yet so connected to my own island roots. I continued to go to church on Sunday mornings, but I really worshipped on Sunday nights.

The Spiritual Realm

Not only were the worship and theology I encountered in America different from what I was raised with, the underlying worldview and presuppositions about reality were challenged. The very foundation and fabric of the world I thought I understood seemed to be attacked at every turn.

In PNG it was just taken for granted that the unseen spiritual world and the physical world were intimately connected. I grew up hearing all sorts of wild stories told by different missionaries about seeing and experiencing the mystical: demons, angels, ghosts. I was amazed at tales of men and women walking into invisible walls unable to pass, or seeing people lifted off the ground and transported across a room as if lifted by an invisible hand. My own father had a couple of experiences when he woke up with a suffocating weight on his chest like he was being crushed to death while a set of red eyes hung in the air above him, staring at him. Barely able to speak, he managed to whisper the name of Jesus and suddenly he was freed.

The most stunning stories came from the Papua New Guinean people themselves. For centuries they have been worshipping the spirit realm and are much more in tune with the unseen than we Westerners are. One of my father's friends was the son of a powerful witchdoctor who was deeply involved with spirits and demons. He had an entire room filled with idols and attached to each of these was a demon with a different sort of power he harnessed: healing, fertility, curses, etc. He used these demons to acquire wealth and power. His reputation reached far and wide, and the neighboring people lived in constant fear of him.

Surprisingly, the witchdoctor decided to send his son to the local Christian missionary school to receive a good education. There, his son learned about Jesus along with his reading and writing instruction and eventually became a Christian. Instead of following in his father's footsteps, he decided to cast out the demons his father used to control and manipulate people. He boldly went into the room filled with hideous idols and in the powerful name of Jesus commanded the spirits to leave. The demons were forced to flee and he broke his father's dark hold over that area of the country. It wasn't long before a large Christian revival started in the area, led by my father's friend. After years of oppression and darkness there was a sense of freedom. The people clung to Jesus as the One who sets the captives free, the One who brings light into darkness. This was just the beginning of many miraculous happenings. After hearing this man tell his story, you could tell it wasn't just the sort of thing you could discard as hearsay. This wasn't gossip or rumors. It was his life.

I compiled all these stories from the people around me who I knew and trusted, and without realizing it, they helped to mold my worldview. They created room for ambiguities and options I quickly realized most people were not open to when I returned to America. Talk of demons and spirits and ancestor worship made people uneasy. In my world of Biblical studies in college, plenty of folks thought I'd gone off the deep end.

My experience of the spiritual realm was not totally gleaned from stories. In high school I began to have strange dreams and to be paralyzed with fear for no logical reason whenever I entered my room. The fear was so strong as soon as I stepped through the door; it was like I was suddenly being enfolded in a thick black coat. In my dreams I began to see myself staring into a mirror looking at my reflection, and then suddenly my face began to contort until staring back at me was the horrific face of a demon. I would wake up shaking with a sense of darkness and evil all around me.

This went on for some weeks before I said something to anyone. I told myself I was overreacting, and it was all in my mind, but the dreams became more and more frequent instead of going away. I began praying, but even that didn't make any difference. I felt embarrassed to ask for help. I was ashamed something like this was happening to me, and I wasn't spiritually strong enough to beat it by myself.

Finally I told my parents. They immediately rounded up the elders of the Pidgin church to come in and pray over my room and over me. They did not think I was crazy or that I was just making up stories for attention. Those short, stocky men walked into our house and began to pray. They anointed my room with oil. They were spiritual warriors of unparalleled power. Whatever demons had been plaguing me fled and I never had any problems again. It was a truly humbling experience as I watched and learned from them. Many times I have gone back and replayed that afternoon in my head, remembering how they held hands and prayed as a symbol of unity, the way they proclaimed the name of Jesus with such deep love and authority, and the care they took in explaining to me what they were doing so that I might understand.

Having been raised in this environment, I just assumed everyone believed in the spiritual realm and things like angels and demons. You can imagine my surprise when I went to college and started having conversations with people only to find out they didn't believe in things like angels and demons or speaking in tongues. Most of my Christian friends thought such things were basically old wives tales and were for uneducated people. I shared my stories with them only to draw forth strange looks or the old shake of the head and the condescending put-downs like "I don't know, man. It all sounds a little far-fetched to me." And just like that, they shrugged off everything I said because it didn't fit into their neat scientific worldview. There was an ingrained rigidity against unquantifiable things. They were unwilling to entertain the possibility of a vast reality beyond our control. So I stopped telling my stories about the spiritual realm because people looked at me like I was crazy and unintelligent, and as an insecure college student I wasn't terribly fond of this. But underneath the silence I still believed. Today I believe more than ever.

Encounter

In 10th grade when we were home on furlough I joined a Christian group and was invited to their regional winter retreat. I was so excited! This was my first American retreat. I came prepared with my Bible, and I had my journal and multiple pens ready for taking notes. Much to my surprise I was the only student with a Bible, and soon I realized why. Almost the entire retreat was filled with strange games and loud songs I'd never heard. To my horror, many of the songs were not even Christian! I was very confused. I thought this was a Christian retreat. Why did everyone seem much more interested in scouting out cute guys and girls from other groups instead of learning about faith? This was all so foreign from what I thought I was getting myself into.

Once a year in PNG there was a weeklong spiritual retreat for students in 9th through 12th grade. As a young kid, I salivated at the thought of growing up to be old enough to go to Encounter someday. It was a coming-of-age experience, the line in the sand separating the kids from the mature young adults. Being a part of Encounter was like being a part of special club. Technically, Encounter was not mandatory, but if you didn't go you were basically an outsider. So everyone went.

When I look back on my time growing up as an MK I feel like Encounter in many ways captured the whole

MK experience in a tiny weeklong nutshell with its intense community and its serious focus on Christian growth. From the time we loaded the beat-up busses and vans and started bouncing down the road singing worship songs at the top of our lungs while sharing snacks, we were like a giant family. Crammed in together, we didn't complain about the choking dust and the body odor. There was a profound sense of solidarity and community as we embarked on this fabulous physical and spiritual adventure.

If you ever attended a Christian summer camp here in the States, take the spiritual intensity of that week and multiply it by about 100 hundred and you will have a little taste of Encounter. The speakers were treated like rock stars—like foreign prophets sent by God into our midst. We listened to each of their talks with baited breath, furiously scribbling down notes for fear we might miss something God wanted to say to us. When it was time to worship we gave the heavenly choir a run for their money in terms of sheer volume. We jumped up and down, moshed and waved our hands, singing as loudly as we could along with the band, while one poor soul stood in the midst of the chaos trying to work the overhead projector.

The feeling in the room was so electric it made the hair on our arms and legs stand on end. Students gave their life to Christ with public declarations and the students watching went wild. Others of us rededicated our lives to Christ with renewed passion and vigor, and there were adults up front to pray with us and for us. I left those meetings simultaneously spiritually charged and emotionally exhausted. Throw in some severe sleep deprivation, because we stayed up far too late talking and praying in our cabins, and you had a recipe for a wild and crazy week.

When the week had run its course we all piled back into the vehicles and headed home, a little less energetic. We returned to a community eagerly waiting to see what God had been up to. The first Sunday night after we returned there was a special Encounter service where the whole community piled into the largest building on our mission base, the meetinghouse, to get a little taste of Encounter. The band played and, still on our spiritual high, many of us students crowded to the front of the room dancing and singing, still holding on to the fiery fervor. When the last notes had faded and the last of us young people stopped yelling things like "I'm gonna be a history maker in this world!" there was an open mic for students to share their experiences at Encounter.

This was the time when everyone waited for the wayward, fringe MKs who had given or re-committed their lives to Christ to come forward. I know this may sound terrible, but I always sensed that people wanted to see the "bad" kids transformed. They wanted to hear about the miraculous. I struggled and continue to struggle with this focus because I feel we in the church continue to emphasize the extreme. The night was quickly filled up with stories and revelations, tears and laughter as student after student shared. When time had run out and everyone had drunk their fill of emotional stories, the band came back for one final anthem, sending us all into the night trying to hang onto the euphoria for just a little longer.

I was always one of the "good" kids and felt like my story was unimportant because I didn't smoke pot and skip Sunday school, because the spiritual things taking place in my own life were somehow less significant because they didn't come with a wild back story or radical conversion experience, because they weren't "juicy" enough. I still went up to share in front of the community from time to time, but when I did there was always a twinge that perhaps I was stealing time from someone else who had something more important and radical to say. I learned to long for the spectacle or the extreme, and because I didn't fall into either of those categories it was as if something in my own spiritual journey was lacking.

I wonder now how the "troubled" students felt: the ones the rest of us were worried for. Nothing was really ever said, but we all knew who they were. No scarlet letters were necessary. What was their experience of Encounter? Did they think we were all just a bunch of crazy Jesus worshippers who might drink the Kool-Aid at any moment?

The Jesus Video

I found myself lying on the floor of a large round hut, exhausted from a grueling day of hiking up and down mountainous terrain. A massive storm followed us into the secluded village pounding down on the thatch roof. Our mishmash team of adult leaders and high school guys were on a mission to share the Jesus video in the native language of one of the most remote people groups around.

It had been a long and bumpy road to get to this point. Literally! We crammed into a couple of four-wheel-drive vehicles and took them way back into the mountains. The roads turned to dirt paths that eventually gave way to impassable terrain clearly not designed for cars. When the ruts in the road became so deep that you could lie down in them and disappear from view, we knew it was time to walk.

Carrying our backpacks filled with a set or two of extra clothes and bags of rice and other food to eat along the way, we started up the steep incline ahead of us. It wasn't long before the straps in my backpack began to dig into my sides and the one-kilo rice bags began to feel like dumb bells. Up, up and up we walked.

A couple of the local villagers joined our group and offered to help carry the gear. One of the men, built like a bull, carried the generator on his back that we would use to show the Jesus video. Another carried the oversized containers of gasoline to run the bulky machine, while I struggled with my little pack.

We hiked for hours, and I rationed out the bag of jelly beans I'd brought along with me while trying to bum beef jerky off my friend, Garrett. The first night we shared the Jesus video sitting in a rugby field with knee high grass. The generator hummed in the background as the Jesus story unfolded on a white sheet we'd set up between two soccer posts. The video had been dubbed into the people's language, and there were probably about a hundred men and women and children enraptured as they soaked in every single word of Jesus. Most of them had never seen a TV or a computer, and they certainly had never imagined that God would come to them and speak in their language.

Under a million glistening stars without an electric light for miles, the world was practically aglow, and all the while there was the low hum of the generator as people met Jesus for the first time. The first night felt almost magical.

Four days later as I lay on the floor of the hut the magic was gone. Every single muscle in my body ached. My jelly beans had long ago run out, and I was left salivating over the thought of Ben and Jerry's ice cream as I worked my way through yet another meal of fish out of a tin and rice or sweet potatoes. Let it be noted for the record that I despise fish and loathe sweet potato. And at the end of a long day of hiking the last thing I wanted to do was hear the hum of the generator fire up and watch the nearly three-hour Jesus video one more time in a language I couldn't understand.

So there I was throwing myself a pathetic little pity party as people piled into the hut where we were staying. Like sardines in a can, they just kept squirming their way in, finding space where I would have sworn no human could possibly fit. One of the leaders stood up and introduced the video, and then the familiar hum of the generator started up again.

I lay down behind the screen and closed my eyes. The pounding of the rain on the roof drowned out the sound of the generator and, for the most part, the ongoing garbled dialogue of the video. I drifted off to sleep wishing that I'd brought ibuprofen.

I was sitting down at an all-you-can-eat buffet when I heard someone crying. It was a low mournful sound, and I looked around but couldn't see anyone. I went back to eating when I heard the sound again, but this time it was joined by a high-pitched voice. The two voices slowly crescendoed, as they were joined by more sorrowful cries of anguish. The entire room full of people began to shake, unable to contain their grief.

My eyes popped open and I was disoriented. The buffet was gone but the voices were louder than ever. I looked through the fuzzy images on the sheet and saw Jesus being scourged mercilessly. The leather lash bit deep and blood flowed down his back like red ribbons. Beyond the fuzzy screen I saw the dark room filled with teary eyes as the villagers cried out on behalf of Jesus, sharing in his pain.

The hut erupted as the metal spikes were driven through Jesus' hands and he writhed in pain. There were shouts of anger and protest as if they were first century witnesses to this atrocity. Their shouts and cries and tears ran together into a song of sacred sorrow when Jesus hung his thorny head and breathed his last. It was like one of their very own had died. The wailing surged and crashed like a mighty wave breaking over our small hut. Then silence filled the space, deep silence that said more than words could have. The rain petered out. Like the villagers, the earth had no more tears to shed.

I sat, eyes riveted on these beautiful people. My soul was torn open and filled with their tears and their anguish. I saw the story as if for the first time when I saw it through their eyes. They welcomed me in and gave me the most beautiful gifts. As the tears rolled down my cheeks, I waited with baited breath. The story was not over.

Jesus showed up, and the people's sorrow turned to dancing. They shouted and laughed and wiped tears from their red, runny eyes. In those cramped quarters people leapt to their feet and others raised their hands in triumph. Jesus was alive. The lover of the lost and the lowly and the forgotten had come to these common villagers isolated from the rest of the world, and speaking their language, he dared to share his story with them.

Many times I have gone back to that hut, tucked away in the mountains cloaked by rain clouds. When my reading of the Bible is like watching old re-runs and my prayers feel forced and dry, I close my eyes and return. I see it all again. The faces, the bright eyes and the tears, and I am reminded that Jesus is far more beautiful and for more enticing than I have allowed him to become. I am forced to confess that I have made Jesus very small, and I try to be surprised by Jesus all over again.

Heaven on Earth

During my senior year, a group of missionary students traveled down to the coastal town of Madang for a mission trip. When Sunday rolled around we piled into our big blue bus to visit a local church. Much to my surprise, when we pulled up to the building the national people were setting up tarps outside in the grass for people to sit on. As soon as we stepped off the bus everybody swarmed around us shaking hands and saying hello. It was the ultimate hospitable welcome. We were immediately invited to join the youth group kids who were leading worship, and by invited I mean we really had little choice in the matter. We grabbed mics and guitars and hopped in.

I was rather skeptical of the whole thing. I was tired after a week of hard work and had been to enough PNG services to know there was no one-hour time cap. They tended to run really long, and here we were outside in the blazing heat with an ancient sound system and out-of-tune instruments with a group of people we'd never met before. The regulars began to fill up the tarps, and as they did, to my amazement, the Holy Spirit arrived with them.

As we began to sing together without hymnals or pews or even a roof over our heads, the joy of the Lord descended upon us like a cloud. Suddenly, we felt as if we had been transported into the very throne room of heaven. There amongst our Papua

New Guinean brothers and sisters in Christ we worshipped with all of our hearts and all of our strength. Everyone was up on their feet clapping and dancing, and tears of joy were flowing like a river. It was a perfect picture of the multitude of people from every nation and tribe and people and tongue and joining together in praise described in Revelation 7:9. There we were, strangers gathered in a field for just a short time, never to see each other again on earth, and yet we shared in a holy and eternal moment. Together we glimpsed heaven in its beauty and its mystery.

For a few hours we experienced Heaven on earth. There was abundant joy without the gimmicks of games and lights that too often accompany Christian mountain top experiences. There was no bait and switch. There was no one carefully crafting the program to produce a certain religious experience or set of emotions. We were just people sitting in a field together surrounded by the God who loved us, and that was all we needed.

When people ask me why my parents would give up a good life to go overseas I tell them this story. When my heart breaks knowing that in just a few precious months my parents will be leaving for three years and will not be present for my son's life I remember this story. When people ask if I had a choice would I go back and do it all over again I remember this story and without hesitation I say, "Yes."

Chapter 6
Much to Learn

It is so easy as people of privilege from the Western world to approach missions from a place of pride. How simple it is to fall into the mindset that we are going out into the world to save the heathens. We are the good samaritans sacrificing our time and talents to help the lowly and impoverished people of the world. Missions can quickly become about us and what we bring to the table. Missions can degrade into an exercise in egotism that blinds us to the deep spiritual poverty within our own souls. I believe with all my heart that the Holy Spirit is at work in all the world cultivating good soil in the hearts of people long before they hear the name of Jesus. It is no surprise to me that we have so much to learn from our brothers and sisters around the world about love and grace and community.

A Fisherman's Tale

Every culture has different forms of community, places and reasons for people to come and share life together. In America we gather over holidays, sporting events and potlucks. I love all of these things, but there is something superficial about these experiences. They aren't "real life." We come together to forget about the everyday grind. Community generally occurs when we are removed from the ordinariness of daily life.

It is no wonder to me that "community" has become a buzzword in the church. If you want to help a program become popular, claim that it creates "authentic community." Ask people to leave their homes and natural environments, feed them some food and, VOILÀ, you have community! I just wonder if we have a little something to learn from the Senegalese about "authentic community."

Our family lived a couple hundred yards from the ocean. Just a thin strip of sand separated us from the Atlantic. Daily we woke up and went to sleep to the sound of the waves crashing and the surf washing up on shore. Early every morning Senegalese men got into their boats and went out over the waters in search of fish. Now these were not the typical fishing boats you and I probably envision. The men would go out in narrow wooden canoes, the sort of canoes in which one person shifting his or her weight too much could capsize the whole thing. They would go far out to sea in search of marlin and tuna and even swordfish. As they rowed back home at dusk trailing their large nets filled with fish, all the people from the surrounding neighborhoods would come out to help haul in the catch.

Huge ropes were tossed to those on the beach, and together the community heaved and tugged on the line, pulling the men, their boats and their flopping nets through the breakers to shore.

Meanwhile, all of us children would scamper around in and out of the legs of the hard-working adults. When feeling brave, we added our tiny muscles to the group's efforts by grabbing onto the very end of the rope and straining with all our might, pretending we were the ones doing all the work. Of course, we soon grew tired of pulling and began to run about, again causing mischief. In our own small way we too played a part in the community.

When at last the boats had been pulled ashore along with the nets, things really got exciting. The families of those who had helped would begin to divvy up the immense haul of slippery silver fish flopping about in the sand with their big, unblinking eyes. They were all different shapes and sizes, and yet somehow in the midst of the chaos the people knew exactly who should get what. Watching the people move about, everybody playing his part, was like observing a magnificently choreographed dance. This was a truly communal event, a ritual of connectedness learned across the generations and passed down as the villagers all worked together for survival.

All the women brought big buckets down to the shore in which to place their prized fish. Then, right there on the beach, they sat in the sand with their fresh wares and instantly a fish market appeared! The sellers marked a few fish to take home for dinner, but the rest were ready to be sold to the highest bidder as folks wandered down to the impromptu market to buy the catch of the day for their regular dinner of fish and rice. Soon there was the sound of fish being scraped and chopped, and fish guts flew in all directions. Glittering fish scales covered everything in a silvery sheen. Voices were raised and heads wagged back and forth as people haggled over the price of fish.

These hungry folks were not the only recipients of a prize. On the occasion when a swordfish or two was caught, the adults chopped off the long, pointed swordfish noses and gave them to us kids. Oh, what a magnificent treasure swordfish noses are. They magically transformed into lances and we would fight and battle with them, pretending to be Robin Hood or Peter Pan until someone got hit a little too hard and erupted into tears. Then they became javelins and we hurled them like the mighty Greek warriors of old. When we were tired of being soldiers, they turned into walking sticks and canes as we hobbled about, suddenly old and crippled. There were endless possibilities to be realized with a swordfish nose. We considered ourselves to be like princes, lucky to have such a wonderful toy with which to play. We did not know we were poor. Our lives were rich with imagination as we experienced the joys and wonders of simplicity.

African Hospitality

I have heard my mother say on numerous occasions that our African neighbors would often come and take us away for hours at a time, and she had no idea where we were. Here in America we probably would have been on the missing children's list, but things are different in Africa where everyone is part of the family. Though surprising to most Americans, life was much safer there.

When we moved into our new home in Dakar we lived in a first floor apartment attached to a home owned by a wealthy government official, a powerful man in the community. Upon our arrival, his wife, Radi, dressed in her finest clothes and marched all around the neighborhood introducing our family and in not so many words informing them not to bother the toubabs (white people). Radi was not the sort of woman you crossed, and the message was heard loud and clear. Nobody ever harmed us, and we were free to pretty much go and do as we pleased.

In fact, my brother, sister and I were treated like demigods. There was no end to the lavish hospitality we experienced from our neighbors. They would go hungry to ensure that we had food to eat. All the people loved us because of our white skin, bleached blonde hair and chubby cheeks. In Senegal the people have beautiful ebony skin, but there is a stigma against being dark. Sadly, the women, especially, often try to lighten their skin using expensive creams. As a lingering result of European colonialism, light skin is considered superior, while in the West we light skinned people are always trying to get tanned and look darker. It seems like nobody is ever content with who they are.

Our neighbors were especially enamored with my little brother, Landon, who was the cutest little baby you can imagine. Every day for lunch he received his own specially prepared dish of African food. In fact, he became so spoiled that he'd refuse to eat the food my mother made for him. Instead, he would wait for his platter of freshly cooked Senegalese food, which he would wolf down upon arrival. Our neighbors took great joy in Landon's appreciation for their cuisine although my mother was sometimes puzzled as to why he preferred their food over hers.

Food etiquette in Senegal is quite different than in America. There you all eat out of the same giant metal bowl, eating strictly with your hands. It's a wonderful thing, really. Think of all the dishwashing saved. Sitting on the floor around the bowl, everyone digs into the mound of steamed white rice using their right hand. You won't find left-handed people in Senegal—your left hand is considered unclean because it's the hand you use to wipe when you go to the bathroom. For most of us that wouldn't be a problem, but for my dad, who's a lefty, it certainly took some getting used to.

While at our American dinner tables there is often a jumble of confusion passing different plates and dishes and sauces around, the Senegalese don't have this problem. There is one simple rule: you eat only from the section of the bowl in front of you. This could be very frustrating if you looked at your section of the bowl and realized you had only a few small morsels of meat while those around you were loaded up with delicious chicken legs or healthy portions of fresh fish. Even then, no shifting of the bowl was allowed; you had to eat the food placed before you. Of course, our neighbors always made sure we kids had plenty of meat. We were always given the best. Oh yes, we were spoiled.

The actual act of eating was a bit of an art. First of all, you had to know what food you could and could not eat. The Senegalese like their food spicy, very spicy. So as foreigners not used to this amount of heat, we had to be careful not to eat the peppers or other spicy stuffing they used in some of their dishes. Secondly, you had to be on the alert for small, sharp fish bones since they cooked their fish whole. If you were really brave you could eat the fish head, and if you were feeling extremely adventurous you could eat the eyes. Fried fish eyes were considered a delicacy. Once you knew what was and wasn't okay to eat, it was time to dig in.

Reaching into the bowl you pull out a small handful of rice, and then tactfully ring out the orangish grease, making sure not to drip any on your neighbor or on someone else's section of the bowl. This may sound simple, but believe me, it is an acquired skill. Finding a way to lift the little ball of rice and sauce into your mouth is quite a feat, otherwise you end up licking your own hand. Many an intelligent missionary has looked foolish on their first attempt.

When all the food was eaten, there was still one more foodie adventure to be enjoyed. My favorite part of the Senegalese culinary experience was eating what we called "cruk cruk." This was the thick, partially burned rice at the bottom of the huge metal pots. This rice always had a wonderful crunchy feel to it. Eating "cruk cruck" is my first food memory. It's no wonder I've always been a texture person when it comes to food.

Along with their immense bowls of spicy rice, the Senegalese loved to drink coffee, but this was not your average cup of Joe. They took coffee to a whole new level! Senegalese drink their coffee in big pink plastic cups filled half way with espresso which they top off to the brim with evaporated milk. Each cup is then doused with enough sugar to make a Southern sweet tea lover blush, and there you have it: the perfect cup of Senegalese coffee. You can keep your Red Bulls and five-hour energy drinks. I'll take a big pink cup of this coffee concoction any day.

My parents were very careful about what types of food and drink we had in the house while growing up. Only on birthdays and rare occasions was Coke or candy or coffee in the house. You can imagine my mother's astonishment when she walked into the neighbors' house one day and found my sister and me with our giant cups of this hyper-caffeinated, sugar-saturated Senegalese coffee. But what takes the cake is that my baby brother was also being spoon fed his own dose of the heavenly brew. It didn't take long before my mother heard the whole story from the neighbors. Apparently they had been feeding us coffee since we arrived, and by now all three of us were thoroughly addicted. To this day I cannot drink coffee without an unhealthy amount of cream and sugar. For this I have my African neighbors to thank.

A Long-Awaited Apple Pie

Living in a culture outside your own, there is no way of avoiding the uncomfortable interactions that happen when the differences in cultures collide. My father experienced this first-hand with my sister.

One day my fair-skinned, blonde-haired sister was prancing about in a smocked summer dress. Smiling ear to ear as a bubbly six-year-old angel, she was the ideal of African beauty. My father was walking with her at one of the local boutiques when he was approached by a young Senegalese man.

"Excuse me, sir, is your daughter available?"

You can imagine my father's curiosity as to what this unexpected question meant.

"What exactly do you mean?"

"Does she have a husband?"

"Well, no. She is only six."

"Good, I would like to marry her."

"She's too young for marriage."

"No problem. I will wait."

"Oh. Why are you so intent on marrying her?"

"I have always wanted apple pie."

"What?"

"Yes, if I marry an American woman, then she can make me apple pie whenever I want. Do not worry; I will pay you well for her."

"Umm…I'm sorry but she's not for sale. Thank you."

And that was the day my father missed out on a great moneymaking opportunity but managed to save my sister from a lifetime of making apple pies for her husband. Apparently marrying for love is overrated these days, but marrying for apple pie—now that sounds like a deal.

An Odd Pet

My father was born to be a missionary. As a kid he was a yard sale fan and a coin collector always looking for a deal. He had no idea those hobbies were preparing him for the skill of incessant bartering and haggling over everything in Senegal.

Dad trudged through the thick Senegalese sand as the gusting ocean winds tugged and pulled at his clothes, much like the small children begging for alms. He made his way along the beach past the rows of small cement houses crowded with our African neighbors. His final destination, like the rest of the landscape, lay under the looming gaze of the giant domed mosque.

From a distance, the little market looked like nothing more than a row of ramshackle stalls barely holding together. Long before you reached them you walked into a wall of fish stench so powerful it made your nose burn and your eyes water. Inside the market there were piles of fish laid out on display staring up at you unblinking in the intense heat. Their scales reflected the bright sun like a thousand tiny mirrors. Flies swarmed everywhere, a buzzing black cloud constantly on the move. Other vendors stood beside 50-kilo bags of rice—long-grain, short-grain, hard-grain rice. Who knew so many varieties of rice existed?

Cutting through the flies, the voices of the vendors all mingled together as they called out their wares trying to get my dad's attention. Underneath the yelling was the low rumbling of bartering taking place with other shoppers. A half cow hung from a red stained rope. Drops of blood slowly dripped into the sand. The shopkeeper fanned the carcass with an old newspaper in a half-hearted attempt to keep the attacking flies away. It was a losing battle.

Live chickens were stuffed squawking and scuffling into wire mesh cages. Raucous hooligans, they said their final good-byes to this world for all to hear before being decapitated and plucked for dinner. Dad wove his way through this maze unfazed by the chaos. He fit right in.

Along with the day-to-day shopping, my father had a knack for coming home with some unexpected treasures. On one occasion he sauntered home with a mysterious new pet. Riding on his shoulder was a spiky, color-shifting chameleon. With its big eyes, crested head and scaly skin, the critter looked like it had just emerged from the prehistoric era. I was fascinated by this strange creature. Dad put the little guy out in the courtyard where he would live amongst the vines hanging from the walls.

Now the chameleon presented a unique type of problem. My sister and I could never seem to find him. He blended in so well that after a few minutes of searching without success we would just give up.

Perhaps my parents should have invested in something simple, clean and easy to find like a goldfish.

Shortly after we welcomed the chameleon into our family, my father decided to show off our cool pet to the neighbors. He placed the reptile on his shoulder and walked into the neighbor's house. As soon as the ladies saw the chameleon they screamed and started running away from him. We heard the sudden sound of doors being locked and bolted, and within a matter of seconds we were standing all alone in the long hallway—not exactly the response my father had been expecting.

The women pleaded with him through the barricaded doors to take the bedeviled thing out of the house. They claimed the chameleon was, in fact, possessed by demons. How else could it change colors? They swore if it bit them they would die instantly, and it seemed they were not quite ready for the afterlife.

My father tried to talk some sense into them by letting them know he'd already been bitten multiple times and was still breathing. He was even willing to demonstrate for them. "It's because you're white!" they yelled. "It can't kill you because you're white." My father is not one to easily admit defeat, but it was quite clear these religious ladies were taking no chances. I didn't really know what demons were, but the fact that my new pet could kill people with a single bite was pretty cool. We kept him around until one day he just disappeared once and for all.

One Tough Granny

My father may have been born to be a missionary, but even he made a few mistakes along the way. One of them has become a family favorite that he will never live down, but let me give you a little background first.

Traditionally, PNG men were responsible for hunting and protecting the village from neighboring people groups who might attack. This left the women to do most of the gardening. Now when I talk about a garden I don't mean a little rinky dink cluster of tomato plants in the back yard. Imagine a small farm-- that's more like it. And the people didn't have any fancy John Deere tractors to make life easy for them. Their farming methods were the same time-tested techniques of their ancestors passed down from generation to generation with little change. The tools they had available to work with made the Amish look technologically advanced, but they were tireless workers.

PNG women are made of iron forged in a fire far hotter than most of us can imagine. Though many of them stand not much taller than five feet, they are tough and they work the land with their hands just like they have for centuries. Now if this doesn't sound hard enough, where we lived in the mountains, most of the fields were on steep hillsides. All day these ladies would walk up and down the hillsides in the sun digging and planting and gathering. Most of them would be growing sweet potatoes. It's hard for us to imagine, but day in and day out the people usually eat sweet potatoes for breakfast, lunch and dinner.

All these hard-working women carry string bags called bilums. Each bag is handmade and takes weeks or months to complete. Their vibrant colors and patterns are some of the most beautiful examples of native artistic expression. At the end of the day, the women will fill up a large bilum or two with sweet potatoes and any other ripe vegetables. By the time their bilums are filled, they can weigh upwards of 80 pounds. The women then place the strap of the bilum around their forehead, bearing the full weight of the load with their necks. It is a remarkable thing to watch these tiny women hoist bilums weighing probably more than half their body weight onto their head and then carry it a couple of miles to their home. Who needs a gym membership when you have to do that every day?!

One day our family was visiting some friends who lived in a house close to the top of a very steep hill. We were sitting outside minding our own business when a little old lady came walking around the bend with such a big load of firewood in her bilum that she almost disappeared under the sheer size of her cargo. She stopped to say hello to us and take a little breather. When she smiled you could see she had only a few broken teeth left and her skinny arms were covered in wrinkly skin. She had to be at least 60 years old. She told us she did this trek every day and that her house was just a couple of minutes away.

Feeling sorry for her, my dad offered to carry the firewood the rest of the way to her house. She nodded her head "yes." My dad, forever the knight in shining armor, grabbed hold of the bilum's shoulder strap to pick it up. He pulled, flexing his biceps with great effort, but the bag barely lifted off the ground. He tried a second time, heaving and straining with all his might, but for the life of him he could not do it. Oh boy, I thought the old lady might start rolling on the ground laughing.

My dad was flustered. This was not exactly how this whole scene had played out in his mind. The old woman was grinning ear to ear with her toothless gums on full display as she stooped down and, in one motion, stood up with the bilum on her back. With a smile and a jerk, that itty-bitty PNG grandma had completely showed up my father.

Nursing Mother

We stepped into the darkness of the grass hut with its walls made out of thick woven grass and a thick thatch roof to repel the rain. There were no windows to let in the sunlight. The floor was nothing more than the brown Papua New Guinean soil swept clean with a makeshift broom. In the middle of the round hut sat an open fire pit where sweet potatoes were being roasted in the hot coals. Welcome to the typical PNG kitchen.

Seated beside the fire on a homemade wooden stool sat a nursing mother. She was not modestly nursing her child under a colorful piece of material. No, in true PNG fashion her long saggy breasts were there for all the world to see. It was clear as they dangled down to the middle of her chest that this was not her first time. She did not so much as blink as we walked in. Breasts are not considered a sexual part of the body in PNG culture, and once you have seen enough breasts like hers bobbing about, you can understand why.

Shortly after we arrived the mother lay the milk-drunk child down on a mat beside her and smiled at us. A tiny piglet raced around her feet. It was not unusual for PNG families to keep young pigs in the house to care for them. Pigs were more than cute little pets. They were the family bank account. The more pigs you had, the bigger your bank account. Pigs would be used to barter and trade, and when it came time for a husband to purchase his wife he would pay for her in pigs. Maybe not very romantic, but in a culture where meat is a rare commodity you can begin to understand why pigs were a sign of wealth.

In the blink of an eye, she snatched the piglet up like a falcon. The little pink creature squealed as she cradled it to her chest. Much to my horror she moved beyond the realm of an endearing cuddle with the family pet and latched him on to her breast. I tried not to stare, but it was impossible as he suckled greedily like the estranged twin to the sleeping child on the floor. The mother was making a deposit into the family bank account.

Crabs Anyone?

Wherever you go, there are some things that remain constant, such as the human need to use the bathroom. But the form these bathrooms take can be very interesting. Not having the luxury of modern plumbing, the people of Wuvulu use two types of bathrooms. The first is an ocean toilet. Imagine you are walking out onto a short dock, and at the end there is a small, shack-like structure waiting for you. When you step into the shack you discover a round hole through which you can gaze directly into the ocean. This is what we would call a no-swimming zone. Swarms of small, bottom-feeding fish are hanging around waiting for you to present them with their next organic meal.

The more common bathroom option is what I will affectionately call a long-drop toilet. For those of you who can't figure out for yourself exactly what this means, I will clue you in. This time you are on land, but imagine you are again entering a small shack and there in the ground is a deep, dark hole, the bottom of which you can't make out, and to be completely honest, it's probably better that way. There are swarms of flies buzzing around, and the smell from the pit is not the sort of thing your mind quickly forgets, especially in the heat of the day with the sun beating down on the corrugated iron roof, which makes you feel as if you're in a hot box. Now straddle the hole, drop your drawers and you can figure out the rest for yourself. The house where we were staying had a little outhouse with a long drop, but there was something special about this particular toilet.

The first night I was on the island I crept outside with a flashlight in hand to use the long drop. I was already a little nervous walking out in the dark by myself, and the chorus of insects and eerily waving palm trees had me on edge. When I came to the entrance I undid the latch and watched the warped wooden door slowly swing open on its rusty hinges. Suddenly I heard a strange scuttling sound from within and shined my flashlight onto the ground. There before me sat a crab. This creature was not your average-size crab like you find served at a restaurant. His body was the size of a dinner plate covered in what looked like a reinforced steel shell complete with armored spikes. His beady little eyes gazed up at me angrily, and his powerful pincers were raised in the air, clacking back and forth, ready to attack. He stood his ground, clearly unafraid of me before slowly descending back into the darkness of the pit from which he had come.

That nasty crustacean scared the *omong kosong* right back into me. There was no way I was going to drop my drawers and squat over the open mouth of the long drop and let him pinch my exposed buttocks. No sir. My mama ain't raised no fool. You've got to know when you're beat. The fear of those pincers was more than enough to make me hold it until morning when I would be able to see a lot better. That was the first and last time I tried to go after dark. The guardian of the pit ruled the outhouse at night as far as I was concerned.

When the sun came up I was ready. With a machete in one hand, a roll of toilet paper in the other and a good deal of discomfort in my bowels, I ventured back to the long drop. This was not a battle I could put off much longer, certainly not for our two weeks on the island.

I marched inside with machete raised. My enemy had gone into hiding. I peered down into the pit and saw him far below sitting amidst the squalor. I smiled. It was time. Like an animal in the wild, I took this moment to mark my territory and prove my dominance over my enemy. He might rule during the night, but the day belonged to me.

Pig Hunt

Wild boars are the largest and most dangerous land animals in PNG. For centuries warriors have hunted them throughout the jungles using wooden bows and arrows. The tips of the arrows are carved with sharp notches to ensure they stay lodged in the thick pig hide. The boars are no easy kill. Fast, powerful and ill-tempered, they are quick to attack when they feel threatened. Using their large, razor-sharp tusks like daggers, they have been known to gore men to death. The difficulty of the kill makes both their meat and their tusks prized commodities. The larger the tusks, the higher their value. The people used them to trade like money and would incorporate them into their ceremonial attire as a symbol of wealth and status.

On one occasion I had the opportunity to join in a rather ragtag pig hunt. Armed with spears and bows and arrows, a group of young men from the village set off into the jungle in search of pigs and glory. Amazingly, the locals somehow knew exactly where they were headed in the midst of the dense forest. We came to a small clearing with a number of trees, at the base of which we found a carpet of fallen fruit. The signs they pointed out indicated that a herd of pigs had recently been rooting for the fruit. Apparently this was one of their favorite delicacies. Following the hoof prints, we set out after our prey.

It was made explicitly clear to me that should we sight the pigs, I had one task and one task alone. I was to find a tree and get ready to climb in case one of them charged. The hunters were taking no chances that I would be harmed on their watch. This was one of the many instances while with the PNG people, even though I was born and raised there most of my life, it was clear—I was not one of them. I was different. My white skin and American passport meant I was just a visitor in their world. I was a person of privilege. No matter what I did, I could not bridge that gap. It is just this tension that makes being an MK so difficult. You don't belong in your host country where you live and yet you don't really belong in your home country. Wherever you go you are out of place, a sojourner always stuck between worlds.

After a while one of the boys raised his hand for silence. He pointed toward a nearby tree for me to go sidle up to. Annoyed, I did as I was told. I wanted to have a bow and take a shot, but I knew there was no chance. I was merely an observer. Straining to see through the brush, I could make out a couple of brown bodies in the clearing up ahead. This was it. The boys fanned out, moving as silently as shadows in their bare feet. When everything was ready, one of them whistled like a bird, and arrows flew. There were all sorts of squeals and snorts and then the pounding of hooves. I gripped a low tree branch ready to hoist myself up to safety, but there was no need. The pack had run off deeper into the jungle. At least one of the arrows had found its mark because we could see splatters of blood. Lacking the use of high-powered weapons, the hunters had to exercise extreme patience. Again we tracked down the pigs, shooting at the wounded animal. This time there was no luck—the arrows landed harmlessly around our prey. We were now miles from home and it was late in the afternoon. Even if we caught the pig, carrying it home from this distance, possibly in the dark, would be a long and arduous task. The group decided to call it quits for the day. I was disappointed, to say the least. My first pig hunt was a failure.

As we trekked back dejectedly I couldn't help but think about the great irony of my life as an MK. When I lived in PNG I was a foreigner, and when I moved to America I was a foreigner. Wherever I went, I was a misfit.

Chapter 7
Foodies

When you talk about adapting to a new culture there is no way of avoiding the issue of food. Food is central to every culture, and when missionaries start telling tales there are always bound to be a few good food stories. Not wanting to disappoint, here are a couple of my own.

Sago Grubs

Sago grubs look like short, obese worms with a wrinkle problem. They incessantly squirm about in nasty-looking skin the color of curdled milk. In PNG, where the people have limited access to meat, these juicy little buggers are a perfect protein-packed snack. The ideal way (and I use the word "ideal" here very loosely) of eating these chubby creatures is to skewer a couple on a stick and roast them over a fire and make yourself a crunchy grub shish kebob. Once they are nice and crispy and you have fried all the wiggle out of them, you are ready for a PNG culinary specialty.

For the naturalists, those without a fire or the extremely lazy, there is a second way to eat grubs. The old saying "No Guts No Glory" is especially fitting here, because your other choice is to eat them raw. I was about middle school age walking around the lively market in the big city of Lae when I came across a lady selling grubs. I had never seen so many of them as I stood mesmerized looking at the mass of moving bodies all writhing around in a large blue bowl waiting to be eaten. The sight made my stomach queasy.

The seller noticed my interest and, with a twinkle in her eye, picked out a plump sample. Holding it by its miniature brown head, she offered it to me. I wanted nothing to do with it; but she was insistent, so I took it. It squirmed in the palm of my hand, and I could feel the tiny bristles of hair on its belly rub against my skin. My mouth went dry as cotton.

I sensed that all the national people around me were staring at the little white-skin boy, waiting to see what he would do. I felt the pressure mounting and my stomach tightened into a knot. There was no avoiding it: I had to eat the grub. I closed my eyes and picked it up by its head, dangling it perilously over my mouth. I held it there for a couple of seconds, unable to take the final step. With a shiver, I plopped it into my mouth and bit down. The grub's insides exploded like an oversized fruit gusher. I gagged and then swallowed the whole thing in one giant swallow. I could feel it wriggling all the way down to my stomach. I looked up and the lady was offering me another. As politely as I could, I refused. You could not pay me to eat another live grub. Not then, not ever.

Eggs for Breakfast

There was a small outdoor market where the national people would bring in their produce from the surrounding areas three mornings a week to sell to the missionaries who lived on our center. The market opened promptly at 7:00 a.m. The early bird missionaries would all be standing around the tables with their plastic bags and buckets waiting to be filled. They hovered around the perimeter sizing up the fruits and vegetables available, trying to get a read on different vendors' prices and quality. A prayer would be said to open the market, and as soon as the final amen was uttered there was a mad dash of missionaries hustling in and out amongst the rows of tables laden with fresh leafy lettuce and carrots and all sorts of other organic options. There are few things in life missionaries like more than getting a bargain, so the market was no place for the meek and mild. It was a challenge and a competition. That is why Dad was always the one to go to the market for our family.

Dad came home from the market as usual one morning, and we paid no special attention to him. When we were all sitting down for breakfast, he gently placed an enormous egg on the kitchen table. It was about the size of a Nerf football and must have weighed a couple of pounds. We all just sort of stared at it for a moment in disbelief. "What is it?" I asked.

My father grinned, sporting the sort of half-smile, half-smirk he puts on when he's very pleased with himself. "It's a cassowary egg," he proudly informed us.

I was really impressed. A cassowary is a large flightless bird living in the PNG jungles. These strange-looking birds can grow to be over six feet tall and run 30 miles an hour. They have sharp talons and have been known to kick people to death on rare occasions. So to find a cassowary nest and rob it was quite an extraordinary feat.

"What are you going to do with it?" I whispered.

"I'm going to make some scrambled eggs!" Dad announced.

I grimaced. This was suddenly not so cool. I was not really the adventurous food taster type and it almost seemed wrong to eat such a magnificent object. My mother did not look terribly pleased either. This was not the first time my dad had brought some strange food item home into her kitchen. When they were newly married and living in Colombia, he captured an armadillo and wanted my mother to make soup out of it, but somehow when he turned it over to her the poor creature got away and never found its way into the pot. The cassowary egg was not so lucky.

All three of us kids watched in amazement as Dad carefully cracked a small hole in one end of the egg so he could save the shell. Out poured a big, bright yellow yolk that filled an entire soup bowl! Dad fired up the skillet and scrambled the huge egg just like he had promised. The egg had a slightly unusual flavor, but with a few squirts of ketchup it tasted pretty good. We were really most impressed that it was enough to feed the whole family, including seconds. Now that's what I call egg for breakfast!

Homemade Coffee

Please don't hate me when I tell you a secret: I boycott Starbucks. First of all I can never seem to understand their drink sizes. Since when is the smallest drink option available called a Tall and a medium is a Grande? Umm… Grande means big or large, not average. If that were my only beef with Starbucks, I would probably still frequent them from time to time. But the real issue: I just don't think their coffee is impressive. I can hear the gasps of horror and the sound of readers slamming this book shut, vowing to never touch it again—but hold on. Where I was growing up, coffee was not just some magical commodity that appeared in a coffee shop or in the coffee aisle at the grocery store. We took coffee to a whole other level.

In PNG we had a smattering of about five or six coffee trees growing at the bottom of our yard. Year after year we watched them flower and then produce coffee beans encased in red skins that fell to the ground unpicked. Dad took great pride in our yard and one year decided we were going to try to make our own coffee. When the beans were red and ripe like tiny Christmas bulbs, we picked them straight off the tree. As we worked, we opened up some of the red pods and sucked on the two white coffee beans covered in a sweet slime inside.

Once the beans were in buckets we had to extract them out of their red skins. To start the process, Dad built a little wooden trough where we put the beans so they could sit out in the sun and dry. This period of drying took a couple of weeks. By this time we kids had completely lost interest in the whole project, so Dad was left to do most of the work by himself. After the beans dried, their crusty outer skin still had to be picked or peeled off. This step took hours of prying and rubbing until finally only the pure sun-dried coffee beans remained.

Then came the best part: Dad poured the beans into our large cast iron skillet on the stove in the kitchen and they began to roast, turning into to a deep, rich brown as he stirred. All the while, the most delicious smell of coffee permeated the house. My mother, who dislikes the smell of coffee, would lock herself in the back room, but I would sit at the kitchen table and breathe in as much of the wonderful aroma as possible. Long after the black skillet had been washed and the burners had gone cold, the fragrance lingered in my nostrils and clung to the furniture in a most resilient manner.

The last step was to have the beans ground up in a coffee grinder at our own community store. Now, with the end in sight, we kids were more than happy to take ownership of the project. Dad walked in the door after visiting the grinder with our final product hidden in a plastic bag. He reached inside and pulled out one small bag of coffee grounds and placed it on the table. I kept waiting for more. Surely all of those coffee beans once filling multiple buckets should have made more coffee than that! Our hours of picking and drying and husking had ground down to a single pathetic bag of coffee. That was it. I stared in disbelief, unable to hide my disappointment.

We carefully divided and drank the coffee, "oohing" and "aahing' as if it had been the best brew we'd ever savored, but in all honesty it tasted pretty much like regular coffee. Of course no one admitted it as the coffee steeped and stewed in the industrial strength double-decker coffee pot Dad heated on the stove. We enjoyed every last sip of our precious homemade coffee, drawing it out as long as possible until there was not so much as a coffee ground left. And then, without need for any discussion, we decided never to do it again.

A Little Taste of India

As a junior in high school I embarked on a six-week mission trip to India. Everywhere we went the people always fed us. Since I was incredibly short and skinny, the kind-hearted Indian women made it their personal goal to fatten me up. They would go around serving the different members of my team regular human-sized portions, but when they came to me they would unleash an enormous smile and heap my plate with enough rice to feed a family of giants. I would sit there and smile, trying to be polite while inwardly groaning, wondering where on earth I was going to fit all the food.

There was no hope for passing any of my portions off to a neighbor because all the women would gather around me and watch my every spoonful, urging me on as if I were a half-starved child who was now eating for the first time. I could feel the mountains of rice expanding, pushing against the walls of my stomach. All the while I smiled and kept spooning in more of the evil white grains until I was so stuffed and bloated I could barely get up from the floor where I was seated. I'd trudge around the rest of the day feeling like I had swallowed a bowling ball.

Now had I been dealing with these quantities of American food I would still have struggled, but Indian food has a particular attribute I do not handle well—spiciness. I am an absolute wuss when it comes to eating hot food. So there I was, trying my best to eat all this food while simultaneously trying to deal with the spice factor in front of an audience. Not a simple task when you can barely handle a spicy chicken sandwich from McDonalds.

About midway through our trip I had an especially nasty run-in with a chili at a church meal. The moment I took one dreaded bite I knew I was in for trouble. I had unknowingly chomped down on an innocent-looking chili, and suddenly there was a lava-spewing volcano in my mouth. I swallowed it down, but not before the damage was done. I felt as if I were one of those cartoon characters with steam coming out of his ears. My jaw began to ache and sweat beaded up on my forehead as if I had been pushed into a sauna. I guzzled down my entire canteen of water hoping to wash the painful burning sensation away. Bad decision! It only spread the taste as I swished the fiery water around, making every last inch of my mouth burn uncontrollably. My eyes and nose started running like a faucet and the entire world began to spin. I must have been making some incredibly distressed faces because all the old ladies standing around started laughing hysterically at the poor little white boy who looked like he was about to die.

The only thing that saved me was a small dish of goat curds that, I swear, miraculously appeared on the edge of my plate. They left in their wake a slow burning, like hot coals. Immediately after the food, we went into the church and were kindly escorted to a small, raised platform where we were to sit in front of the congregation. About 20 minutes into the service I knew I was in for trouble when my stomach began to churn and gurgle angrily. This was not going to end well.

Indian services are not like our regular American services. At the one-hour mark they are just getting warmed up. At 60 minutes my stomach moved from continual churning to extreme bowel pain as I sat there cross-legged on the ground, praying to God the pastor would feel the Spirit urging him to cut the service short. No such luck. At two hours I had lost consciousness of what was taking place around me as I focused all of my energy on withstanding my gastrointestinal reflexes. At two and a half hours I began to lose all hope and began to embrace the shame that was sure to be mine; my bowels were in a state of complete rebellion, threatening to explode at any moment. Finally the pastor started praying and the people all bowed their heads. I could wait no longer. Gingerly I picked myself up off the floor and shuffled out of the room as quickly as possible. I had no idea where the bathroom was, but I'd been in India long enough to know what to do. I stepped outside into the alley and, without a hint of remorse, dropped my drawers and felt the final wrath of the chili. At last I was free!

Chapter 8
Brushes With Disaster

Food stories are fun, but near-death stories are even better. In the missionary world, stories are currency. As an MK, having a good adventure story to tell was like rolling into school with a set of brand new designer clothes. When everyone came back from school break there was always the anticipation of new stories and, of course, a little competition to see who just might have the best story to tell. These are a few of my designer clothing stories.

Coral Reef

On the southeast coast of PNG there is a beautiful little lagoon surrounded by a thick wall of coral looking for all the world like a hidden fortress. The fortress, however, has one weakness if you know where to look. Underneath the waves there is a small gap in the coral through which you can swim to the open sea.

A group of us had navigated our way through the secret coral portal and were swimming out in the deep water where the large ocean waves rolled up and down trying to take us with them as they crashed into the coral barrier. Feeling tired after treading water, I decided to head back into shore. Swimming with heavy legs and my snorkel mask on, I approached the reef looking for the hidden passageway. As I drew closer I could feel the waves pulling me in toward the jagged wall.

The bubbles and swirling white water made it difficult to see. At last I found the narrow passage and started swimming into the coral as the sea propelled me forward. I was able to squeeze half my body into the small space before I realized I'd made a terrible mistake. This was a dead end! I tried to push my way out of the enclave but the water was now smashing me into the coral without mercy. I breathed in a mouthful of water through my snorkel and gagged. There was zero visibility and I could feel the salt water stinging the fresh cuts on my hands where I had braced myself against the waves as they threw me against the sharp coral spikes.

Disoriented and scared, I could feel my heart pounding with adrenaline. Not sure what to do and afraid my blood might attract the sharks I'd just seen circling far below us only a hundred yards away, I took action.

Without another thought I hoisted myself up on top of the coral, feeling the pointed spines cut unto my feet like little daggers. One step. Two steps. Three steps. I could hear the crunch of the coral underneath my weight. To anyone watching it must have looked like I suddenly levitated and started walking on the water like Jesus, but I imagine my walking was a little more painful than his.

I dived safely into the ocean on the other side of the coral wall. The coral spikes had managed to break through the thick calluses on the bottom of my feet leaving them raw and bloody. I headed for shore as fast as my weary body would carry me, thankful for having escaped being crushed to death against the coral or becoming shark bait.

Swamp Monsters

The sun was stretching its rays after a long night of sleep, and I was rudely awakened by the rooting of pigs underneath the house and the incessant crowing of a few overzealous crows. I was visiting a friend for the week in the village where his parents were translating the Bible into the local language. Lying in a strange bed, my ears were filled with a hundred different sounds as the world around me gradually came to life.

After a quick breakfast my friends and I stepped out into the village square, an open dirt clearing in the middle of the grass-woven huts—not exactly Main Street. Spotting some of the village boys our age already hard at work, we sauntered over to see what they were up to. We were immediately invited to join them on a fishing excursion. This however, was not your average rod and reel fishing boat charter.

Rather than digging for earthworms and untangling fishing line, the boys were busy pounding piles of poisonous nuts into a fine pulp using hefty stones. The pulp was thrown into an old battered rice bag for safekeeping. Then we all piled into two dugout canoes and started paddling down the river as fast as we could. I was in charge of keeping the smoldering coconut husk at my feet burning so we could start a fire to cook our lunch later. After nearly setting the wooden canoe on fire, I jettisoned the coconut husk into the river. It would be a cold lunch.

After a great deal of paddling and chattering, none of which I understood save for a few phrases here and there my friend translated for me, we arrived at our destination—a giant, slimy swamp dotted with tiny islands. There were strange-looking trees growing up out of the water with huge twisted root systems covered in thick spikes that rose above the murky water level. Though not even midday yet, underneath the canopy of leaves and heavy moss it seemed as if dusk had arrived early.

After we tethered the canoes to a tree and started wading into the swamp, my friend looked at me with a grin and told me, "By the way, sometimes there are crocodiles in here."

"What?!" I nearly turned around right then and there to get back in the boat, but I was too afraid to lose face. Up ahead, the village boys did not seemed bothered by the possibility of gigantic unseen swamp monsters with powerful jaws and razor-sharp teeth emerging out of the murky depths. Armed with only a couple small bamboo fishing spears, they plunged boldly into the swamp. I gulped and started praying we would be surrounded by crocodile-repelling angels. My heart was nearly beating out of my chest as we slogged through the murky water.

I could feel my feet sinking into the thick, cool mud at the bottom of the swamp. It squooshed between my toes with every step. Next thing I knew, I plunged down under the water kicking and thrashing to regain my footing. I surfaced with a face covered in green algae as I swam ahead until I could feel the mud beneath my feet again. Lucky me—I'd found a swamp hole. There were hundreds of these deep pockets all across the swamp, and it wouldn't be the last one I found.

We pushed farther and farther into the swamp and it began to get darker and darker as the trees grew closer and closer together as if they were huddling for support. The village boys started taking the seed pulp and spreading it out over the surface of the water. The swamp fish would eat the poison nuts and die a little while later. When they floated to the surface, the boys would snatch them up to take home. After they'd been cooked, the fish would be perfectly safe to eat.

Scared to death, I was constantly scanning the water looking for anything non-human that was moving. There were plenty of logs and crocodile-shaped objects stuck in the swamp mud to keep my nerves on edge. Every croaking frog and splashing fish made me jump. A large green tree python dangling up above us from a low-hanging limb nearly gave me a heart attack.

At last we emerged from the water and broke for lunch on a small island. There, covered from head to toe in mud and slime, we sat underneath the wild, cascading moss dangling from the overhanging tree limbs in the middle of a giant swamp. There was not an adult for miles around and we had no cell phones or other methods of getting in touch with the outside world. We were completely on our own.

I was gazing haphazardly into the swamp while finishing off the last bite of my sandwich when, for just a split second, I saw a pair of yellow eyes staring at me before they disappeared back underneath the water. I nearly fell off the log I was perched on, and sandwich remnants spewed out of my mouth like confetti.

"Did you see that?" I yelled.

"See what?" someone said.

"The crocodile!!!!"

"You're making things up."

"I most certainly am not. It was looking right at us, probably sizing us up for lunch. I am not going back into that swamp."

"You're seeing things. Plus it's the only way out."

"I don't care. I'm staying right here on dry land."

There was no way anybody was going to get me back into the muddy water with a hungry crocodile lurking nearby.

We all sat staring intently at the surface of the water looking for another sign that we had company, 10 minutes…15 minutes…. Nothing. The village boys were getting anxious. I heard them chattering amongst themselves, and I could guess they were talking about me. I'm sure they thought I was crazy. First I'd ruined the fire and now I claimed to be seeing things.

Nobody else had seen those unblinking yellow eyes, just me, the newbie. No one ever believes the new guy. A group of the boys headed back into the swamp. I waited to hear the sound of chomping and thrashing. Nothing. They waded out of view. The crocodile was probably waiting for me. He, too, sensed I was a newcomer—fresh meat.

My friend Zach spoke up. "We can head back to the village, but you know the only way there is through the swamp."

"I know," I snapped. At any moment I expected blood-curdling screams to pierce the unsettling silence of the swamp as the monster dragged one of the boys under, never to appear again. But still… nothing.

I knew Zach was right, but that didn't make me any more willing to put so much as my little toe in that water again. He handed me a puny fishing spear as if somehow it would do me any good if I were attacked. Armed with my pathetic weapon, I stepped into the water. One step. Two steps. Three steps. I stopped. Were those bubbles coming up to the surface of the water nearby? I froze and raised my spear. This was it—I was going to die!

Then those two yellow eyes re-emerged from the depths. I thrust my spear at them. "Take that, you vicious crocodile!" I felt the spear bite into flesh. I pulled it back for another attack and stopped abruptly. Attached to the end of my spear was my dangerous creature of the swamp: a small dead fish staring at me with big eyes and a mouth wide open as if in a mocking grin. In the background I heard Zach snickering. I felt like an idiot.

Moving as fast as we could, we backtracked through the swamp without further incident. I have never been so happy to see anything in my life as I was when we finally spotted our canoe. The whole trek back up the river I kept replaying the crocodile-spotting scene over and over in my head. Did I really see something? Was I being crazy? Was my imagination playing tricks on me? I guess the answer is, I'll never know.

A Little Storm

PNG gets more rain than anywhere else in the world except for one of the Hawaiian Islands, so we were pretty used to getting tropical rainstorms. One minute it would be bright and sunny, and the next thing you knew huge thunderheads were stampeding over the mountains, rolling across the sky like chariots dragging a thick cloak of darkness in their wake while stirring up swirling winds. As the clouds mounted their charge, everyone fled for the indoors knowing there were only minutes to spare before the storm struck.

One time I was on my way home from the bus stop after another long day in the 4th grade with my oversized backpack swinging back and forth, just minding my own business, when I felt the winds picking up around me, sending a few stray food wrappers swirling into the air. I glanced over my shoulder and saw the rain beginning to come down hard on the hill just behind me with drops the size of marbles. I started sprinting at full speed, trying to outrace the storm, my empty backpack flapping up and down with every step. I could hear the rain pelting the earth behind me but didn't dare to look back. With dust flying at my heels, I rounded a bend in the road and could see my big blue house standing on the corner waiting for me. I couldn't believe it. I was outrunning the rain! I was about 20 feet from the bottom of our yard when a powerful peal of thunder split the air like a sonic boom. It was so loud I instinctively ducked for cover, cowering underneath my bag, which had slid over my head like a black shield.

Suddenly, a second explosion cracked about ten feet in front of me when a lightning bolt struck the road with such force and energy it nearly knocked me off my feet. I froze, in shock, my hair standing on end. I nearly wet myself right there out of sheer terror. I had never witnessed such raw power before. Just a couple more feet and I might have been fried to a crisp or instantly given magic electric superhero powers. Shaking, I just stood there as the pursuing rain caught up to me, soaking me to the bone in an instant. I felt lucky to be alive.

I may have been just a kid, but I have never forgotten that moment—the strange feeling in the air, the smell of scorched earth where the bolt of lightning had struck and the raw irrepressible fear in my gut. Too often in my mind God is small. Somewhere along the way God lost His grandeur. Somewhere in the process of living life and going to church and doing my daily devotional time I became more comfortable with the baby Jesus meek and mild on Christmas cards and the "Jesus is my homeboy" concept. I cultivated an image of Jesus as someone who looks, thinks and talks like me. God the Father became a decrepit old guy with a long white beard looking remarkably similar to Gandalf the White.

But then every once in a while something brings me back to that mind-blowing moment and I am reminded of the truth. We do not serve a weak, aloof God. We bow before the maker and hurler of the lightning bolts who will one day come riding the thunderous storm clouds like a chariot. My story is just a single word, maybe a sentence, in the incredibly story that God is weaving on this planet. If story is currency, then I am grateful to be a part of the most valuable story ever told.

Chapter 9
Rites of Passage

Most of my life was spent at Ukarumpa, which was a world unto itself tucked away in the mountains. Over the years the missionaries from across the world who came and went created rituals to mark the passing of time and to give meaning to our life together. Communal traditions emerged and grew to become more than their creators could have ever imagined. Stories were passed down from one generation to the next, and each year new layers were added to our collective story. Every class left its mark adding to the lore of those who had come before them. These rituals and stories united us and gave rhythm to our strange little world of missionaries. As a kid they built excitement and anticipation, and with each passing year the rituals and stories sank deeper into my blood until I could not separate my story from them. They became the markers that gave my life perspective and context. Ukarumpa was the one place in the world that made sense to me.

Lemon Meringue Pie

It was tradition that each class would do fundraisers to save money for a senior trip. These fundraisers provided much needed entertainment for the community ranging from roller skating nights to the annual Valentine's dinner. My senior year I was in charge of putting on a dessert night fundraiser. Our class had been prepping for weeks, sending out order forms and collecting ingredients and recipes. Saturday, the day of the event, we separated our class of 27 students into different teams. Parents bravely opened up their homes to us and gave us free use of their kitchens to bake all the different dessert options from scratch.

On top of baking desserts for over 200 people, we had to completely transform a number of different classrooms at the high school into elegant dining spaces. With scissors, paper, tinfoil and a whole lot of tape and candles, we went to work. We borrowed and ironed tablecloths and cut and set fresh flowers into vases. We chopped down large stalks of bamboo and brought them in to provide the finishing touch as our English classroom became a five-star, French-style restaurant.

As one of two senior class officers, I spent most of the day running around like a headless chicken making emergency trips to the grocery store and doing other small errands. In the afternoon I was responsible, along with my fellow class officer Haebin, for making all the lemon meringue pies. Now neither of us had ever made a lemon meringue pie and, in spite of going through home economics three times (that's a story for another day), I was still almost useless in the kitchen. Usually I would rely on my mother in these sorts of scenarios, but she was busy, so it was just Haebin, me and mom's homemade pie recipe.

To save time we decided to make all the lemon filling for the pies at the same time. I ran out to the lemon tree in our yard and started squeezing fresh lemons while Haebin started separating eggs. After dumping six times the regular amounts of ingredients in the recipe into a giant bowl, I poured the mixture into mom's largest pot and began to stir it over the stove. Slowly but surely the mixture began to harden as it heated up. Perfect. Soon, however, it began to take more and more effort to maneuver the thick wooden spoon through the gloppy mixture. I was beginning to sweat with effort and then suddenly, with a crack, I snapped the hefty wooden spoon in half. This was not good.

While all of this was happening, Haebin was busy rolling out and edging the most beautiful pie-crusts you have ever seen, completely oblivious to the catastrophe brewing. I, on the other hand, was really beginning to worry. We didn't have enough time or ingredients to start over if this batch failed. I had eaten more than my fair share of lemon meringue pies, and the consistency of our creation was clearly off.

I poured the hot lemony mixture into the first piecrust and it came out slow and heavy like molasses. It was a faded greenish yellow color, not exactly the appetizing canary yellow filling you expect in a lemon meringue pie. I stood there staring, too afraid to touch it and confirm my growing fears. The knot in my stomach was getting tighter with every second.

Just then my dad walked into the kitchen. As a lover of lemon meringues and a true pie connoisseur, he took one look at the pie and his face confirmed my worst fear that something was really wrong. I didn't dare say anything as he scrutinized our debacle. He poked the filling with a fork and it didn't even dent the surface. Not a good start.

He tried to cut it with a knife, and the blade got stuck as if he were trying to cut through half-solidified glue. This was a disaster. As a final test, he used his hands and peeled out the entire innards of the pie in one solid mass. It hung there in the air looking like a ghastly batch of pizza dough waiting to be shaped. Damn! Dad was grinning. "It looks like flubber," he said. I scowled at him. I did not see the humor in this moment.

And then Mom walked in. There was a steep intake of breath and I knew what was coming. "Oh Simeon, you can't serve that to people."

"Well, no freakin' duh! I knew that." Of course, I didn't actually say those words out loud. Otherwise I would have had bigger problems to deal with than a bad batch of lemon meringue pies. Poor Haebin still had no clue what was going on. Lemon meringue pie wasn't exactly a staple dessert in her home country of Korea.

"How many batches did you make at a time, Simeon?" Mom asked.

"All six."

Mom gasped again. "Oh no, you can't do that. Lemon meringues are very fickle. You might be able to make two at a time at the most."

Perfect! Now you tell me, I thought.

We had to start all over again. The race was on. I dashed to the store to buy more ingredients while Dad ran out to our lemon tree to get a fresh batch of lemons. I rushed back and we began whipping up regular-looking batches of lemon meringue pies. When the first set of pies hit the oven I had to run to go make sure setup was on schedule. The clock was ticking. I don't know how they did it, but somehow my parents managed to pull off the lemon meringue pie speed-baking of the century. They showed up just in the nick of time with the pies to fill our first orders as people were being seated.

Oh, and if you were wondering what happened to the failed meringue…well…Dad threw it out into the garden, heaving it like he was doing the hammer throw because the thing was so heavy. It settled in the dirt amongst the plants. When we normally tossed food scraps outside we could pretty much guarantee the scavenging neighborhood dogs would come by and scarf them up immediately, but none of them dared to touch the lemony goo. Not even the torrential Pacific rains could erode the substance. Two weeks later our creation was still there, an indestructible mass to remind me of my failure. To this day I still don't know what went wrong, but we did have some beautiful pie crusts.

Barefoot

I lived my life barefoot, except when our family went to church, and even then as soon as we arrived there, the shoes and socks came off. As a result, my feet were like leather. I would run around on the dirt-covered, rock-strewn roads without a second thought. For fun I would take tacks and see how far I could shove them into my foot before I could feel anything. I played basketball, tennis and soccer barefoot. Shoes were for grownups and pansies. I was neither of those.

One time while hiking in the jungle with my father I stepped on a sharp piece of flint and it snapped off in my heel. I tried to keep walking, but as my feet pounded repeatedly on the hard dirt path the stone dug in farther and farther until it felt like someone was driving a nail into my foot with every awkward step. At last I stopped, unable to keep going because of the pain. We still had miles to go up and down the slippery mountainous terrain before we reached our village destination. Things were not looking good.

Sitting down on the red clay, overshadowed by towering trees covered in serpentine vines and creepers, my father decided to take matters into his own hands. Using the only tool he had available, he calmly pulled a heavy duty Exacto knife out of his backpack. Why in the world he had an Exacto knife just hanging out in his backpack is not a question I thought to ask him at the time, but it strikes me as rather curious now. With hands as steady as a surgeon, my father would have made an incredible doctor if he didn't pass out at the sight of blood. He proceeded to slice about half an inch into my foot using the razor-sharp blade to extract the rock remnant with no warning, no local anesthesia, nothing! The next thing I knew he was holding up the sliver of stone the size of a small arrowhead for me to see. I couldn't believe it—I didn't even know he'd started!

For most kids, the move from elementary school to middle school is a big transition year. Growing up in Papua New Guinea it was just the same for me, but for a slightly different reason. During the holidays before I entered 7th grade, my mother and I sat down for a serious talk. With furrowed brow and solemn voice she informed me I would now have to wear shoes to middle school. Those were some of the saddest words I'd ever heard. This was one tradition I wanted nothing to do with. Sadly I had no choice. My world of barefoot bliss now had to come to an end. No more running about feeling the mud squelching between my toes during recess. My days of freedom were over. Growing up looks like a lot of different things in different places, but to me in my island world it meant having to put on shoes.

Gone Camping

There are many sacred moments on the journey to manhood. One of them is taking on the wildness of the natural world. Of course this step is best when tackled with a tent, a stash of marshmallows and hot dogs, and a nicely rolled sleeping bag. Yeah, even missionary kids don't rough it all the time.

I was in middle school when my friends and I were finally allowed to go camping on our own without an adult. Freedom was ours! The world was our oyster! (I don't really like oysters. In fact, the only time I tried one was while on a retreat. That cold, slimy body slipping down my gullet was nearly enough to make me puke. So what exactly oysters have to do with much of anything, let alone the world, is rather beyond me, but it sounds like the sort of thing sophisticated people would say. As a missionary kid you tend to pick up odd phrases and quotes here and there that you don't fully understand, so let this be a prime example for you.)

It was Friday night and, with enough gear to last probably a couple of weeks, our overburdened and overexcited group headed out into oncoming darkness. In hindsight, we should have picked our campsite and started setting up tents before it turned pitch black, but this is the sort of thing you figure out after you attempt the task with a flashlight clamped between your teeth.

The missions base where we lived was surrounded by a large chain-link fence, so we trekked about a mile to the far edge of the fence and made camp tucked in amongst the waist-high, sharp-bladed grass growing wild and taking over the unoccupied area. Everything was going swimmingly. We gathered wood and proudly started a roaring fire that lit up the night. One of the guys brought along a couple liters of homemade ginger beer, which was a bit of an acquired taste and completely non-alcoholic. But drinking it made us feel like men, so we swallowed and swigged our way through the bottles like a bunch of rabble-rousing pirates downing grog. We all had our pocketknives and whittled away to make the most perfect sticks possible for roasting hot dogs and marshmallows. Basking in the red glow of the warm fire, watching the sparks drift up into the starry night sky as the smell of sizzling hot dogs filled our nostrils, life could not have been any better.

Then it started to rain, just a few drops here and there at first, and we laughed at as they struck the fire with a hiss. But he who laughs last laughs the longest. We did not have the last laugh.

In a matter of minutes we were all piled into the tent along with our gear as the real storm hit. We could hear the rain pounding outside, but we settled down into our sleeping bags and broke out a pack of playing cards to pass the time. Slowly water began to seep into our tent. We all scooched closer together in the middle, trying to avoid touching the outside walls to stay dry. We kept playing cards and it kept raining. The water continued to creep in uninvited to our party. We scrunched even closer together, all huddled in the very center of the tent on the lone remaining section of dry canvas. It kept raining. Crisscrossed and piled on top of each other, we tried to sleep.

We were driven from our half-slumber as our sleeping bags became saturated with water. Every last thing was soaking wet. I looked outside and could see streams of water running alongside our tent. All that remained of our once roaring fire was a pile of cold, blackened sticks. Sopping wet, we were determined not to give up.

We abandoned the notion of sleep, shaking ourselves off like water rats. The rain had now slowed to a light drizzle. Sleepy-eyed, we tried to pass the time talking, but then the dampness of our clothes began to set in. We were all cold and disheveled when at last the rain stopped. We rolled out of the tent and there in the mud we tried to restart the fire, but not a dry piece of wood was to be found. Our precious few scraps of paper were now wadded into a soggy ball. In spite of our grandest efforts we couldn't get a spark to catch. Not even a good dose of kerosene could get the job done. At last we admitted defeat.

As we tore down the tent with the first light of dawn glowing orange and red on the edge of the night sky, it became clear why our campsite had been such a disaster. Foolishly, we'd managed to set up camp in a gully. All the rain had run right down into our tiny little tent like a rushing river. Shivering, we sloshed our way back home with dripping sleeping bags draped over our shoulders and eyes bleary from lack of sleep. We may have been vanquished this time, but we would return to camp another day.

Sunday Night Cards

We always had people coming over for meals when we were growing up. It was just a part of the culture of the Harrar home. When I came home for lunch I never knew who would be there. At least a couple times a week we'd have people over for dinner or games or something. My parents were constantly hosting gatherings and opening up their home to others. My mother bore the brunt of this burden because she did all the cooking. There were no pre-made food options, so week after week she baked and cooked incredible meals from scratch. It was her way of loving us.

My mom and dad had a soft spot in their hearts for the single missionaries in our community because they, too, had started out as single missionaries before courting and getting engaged—via ham radio! The single men especially had a knack for appearing around mealtimes and inviting themselves in to join us for whatever we were having. This never seemed to bother my mother. She'd just go to the refrigerator, grab whatever food we had and put it on the table. No matter what it was, the men always ate it and were grateful. Like stray cats with nowhere to go who just keep coming back, they eventually became part of our family.

Of all the times people came over, Sunday night was the best. Every Sunday night "the men" came over for card night to play pinochle. Over the years the faces at the table changed, but there were a couple of mainstays who stick out in my mind and who stood the test of time. Ben was a quiet airplane mechanic; Christoph who was an energetic Swiss computer whiz; and then there was Lloyd, who I swear, was never dealt a good hand in his life. Dad, who took more risks with his cards than a drunken gambler in Vegas but always seemed to beat the odds, was the final member.

As a young boy I begged and pleaded to stay up long enough to see everybody and watch the first hand. There I'd be in my footed pajamas sitting on Dad's lap looking at his fist-full of cards, listening to the card-playing jargon and trying to make sense of what was going on: spades, hearts, diamonds, clubs; bids and tricks and cards placed upside down in the kitty—it was all so exciting, like learning a new culture with its foreign language and rituals. Dad always made popcorn and started a kettle of hot water boiling for tea and coffee. As I grew up and into a larger size, I passed the footed pajamas along to my brother and was allowed to stay up later and later, always watching and listening and learning.

Then my night finally came. One of the regulars couldn't make it and "the men" had only three players. For years I'd been itching to play, just waiting for my chance. This was my big moment. I was no longer the little kid in footed pajamas. They dealt me in and poured me a cup of steaming hot tea. I was one of them now, one of "the men." My palms were sweaty as I picked up my first hand of cards. I was partnered with my dad. I glanced at him nervously across the table. He was trying to hold back a smirk as he gazed gleefully at his cards. I knew he must have something good. We were going to be okay.

It wasn't long before I was playing more regularly, and by the time I had moved up to high school "the men" would be waiting for me to play when I got home from youth group. There was something sacred about Sunday nights. It was more than the cards and the tea and the slightly salted popcorn. It was about being with those men, being able to listen to their stories. They talked about the beautiful and the mysterious and the mundane. They laughed and dreamed together. At times they even prayed and wept together.

Those men came back week after week, because seated around our card table they were a community. The tea and popcorn were their sacraments, elements just as life-giving as bread and wine. All the stresses and struggles of life disappeared for just a few short hours and they were free. I miss those guys. Most of them have moved, married and had kids. But when I close my eyes I can see them all sitting in their usual chairs, and I wonder if someday in heaven we'll able to play a couple more rounds together.

Banquet

I have held off writing about Banquet until now because it is the most sacred of the Ukarumpa rituals. It is an event with an almost cultic essence. Banquet was one of the reasons missionary kids like Valerie and Bekah returned to PNG. It was the Holy Grail, the most highly anticipated event of our life growing up, awaited with even more excitement than Encounter, because Banquet was for juniors and seniors only.

It was an extravagant affair put on by the parents of these upperclassmen. Every year the parents chose a secret theme and spent the entire year planning and preparing for the event. A few weeks before *the night*, the Teen Center was closed down and the heavy duty work of transforming the entire building into a magical world began. The Teen Center was manned all hours of the day and night as people painted and constructed. A play was written, costumes were sewn and rehearsals were held as the parents prepared a full-length show for the students —all under a great cloak of mystery. No expense was spared, and while the work went on within, rumors swirled without. Everyone tried to guess what the theme was. Students tried to catch snippets of conversations or peer through windows, but the Teen Center was put under lock and key. And that was really just the beginning of it.

Joy and I broke up a month or two before Banquet. There went my date for the big night! This was not good because a lot of the girls had already been snatched up. It seemed like every day I found out that another of the available females had been asked, making the already small pool of options even smaller.

To make matters more complicated, it wasn't enough to just ask a girl. You had to ask with style and creativity. When I was the only one of my close friends without a date, I realized I needed to move fast.

There was one girl left with whom I would enjoy spending an entire evening on this memorable occasion. If she didn't work out I was in serious trouble. Over the weekend I wrote her a cute poem asking her to be my date. I carefully copied the words onto classy parchment paper using a fancy style of calligraphy I found on the internet. I rolled up the parchment to look like a scroll, even going so far as to slightly char the edges, giving the whole thing a vintage look. I placed the scroll in a small bag. It was ready.

Monday morning rolled around and I was nervous, much more nervous than I'd anticipated. I went to school bright and early and hung the bag with its surprise on her locker. All I could do was wait. Mid-morning break couldn't come soon enough. Finally 10:15 a.m. rolled around and I saw Claire. She looked distraught as she walked over to me. This was not good. She was supposed to be happy and excited.

"Simeon, I don't think I can go to Banquet with you."

My heart dropped, but I tried not to show my disappointment. "Okay, why?"

"Somebody asked me on Sunday."

I couldn't believe it. I was a day too late.

I would be going solo. Suddenly the thought of Banquet wasn't quite as exciting.

When I got home my whole family was eagerly awaiting my news and dying to ask me, "How'd it go? Did she like the poem?" I stormed in the door.

"Before you ask," I blurted out, "she said 'No,' she already agreed to go with someone else. I don't even know if I want to go anymore."

I made my way to my room and slammed the door. I stared at my closet. Heck, I didn't even have anything to wear anyway—not a suit, not even a blazer. I'd have to borrow one of Dad's ties. All these years of anticipation and now this whole thing was a debacle.

As the big day drew closer the excitement was ramping up and work on the Teen Center had begun. Even with all the drama I decided that I would go, but sadly I would be going without a date. I heard people talking about how they would make their grand entrance. Every year the whole community came out to see the couples arrive at Banquet, the girls in their elegant dresses escorted by the guys in their suits. People congregated hours before the couples started arriving so they could get a good view.

Most of the couples came in cars freshly cleaned for the occasion, for one night free of the red PNG mud. But the clean cars were nothing compared to some of the extravagant entrances the students planned. Couples rolled up in bathtubs or were carried in on homemade litters like Cleopatra. A couple of times people channeled their inner James Bond by arriving in a helicopter. Every year there were all sorts of crazy ideas. The crowd oohed and aahed at each new couple and clapped especially loud for those who made a clever entrance. It was like being caught in the flash of cameras on the Hollywood red carpet. For one night you were a star.

Just a week or two before Banquet, Joy broke up with her boyfriend. We were still good friends and decided to go together. Now I had a date and the pressure was on because I still nothing to wear. There were no stores where I could go and buy or rent a tux for the night, and I was very short and skinny, so nobody I asked had any dress clothes that would actually fit me. Finally, in an act of desperation I checked out the high school prop room and managed to find an old suit coat jacket, which, while still too large on me, was manageable.

The night of Banquet arrived. Those attending were allowed to leave after lunch to go prepare. For girls this meant hair and makeup. For guys it meant washing cars and procrastinating on getting dressed till the last minute. After what felt like the longest afternoon of my life, I went to pick up Joy.

I stepped out of the car in front of the excited crowd and nervously made my way around to the other side where Joy was waiting. I walked slowly, afraid I would trip and fall and turn the yells and whistles into laughter and humiliation. Joy eased her way out of the backseat and onto the red dirt road without a problem. Whew. So far so good. I gave her my arm.

We started down the roped-off walkway, a stretch of about 50 feet, to our final destination. I reminded myself to move slowly. Joy wobbled beside me in her heels, clinging to my arm as we crossed over the rocky road and onto the grass. The Hollywood red carpet was missing. I did my best to smile as people called our names and set off camera flashes all around us. It took only a couple of seconds for my vision to blur, and I thought I had temporarily gone blind. At last we made it to the end and did a final 360-degree turn and wave. One last explosion of blinding light and we escaped inside, away from the crowds.

Inside, the usual dusty, undecorated room had been transformed into an elegant, Southern-style dining room complete with pillars, a chandelier and a hand-painted fireplace. Small tables with white linens were spread all about and hors d'oeuvres were being served to the couples who had already arrived. We were simple people who would get excited about shipments of American candy once or twice a year. We all wore mud-stained clothes and hand-me-downs. We could fit everything we owned into two suitcases and feel like even that was a little excessive at times. But tonight it was is if somebody had waved a magic wand over everything and we found ourselves in a wondrous fairy tale.

After everyone had arrived and the girls had almost finished oohing and aahing over each other's dresses, dinner began. The food brought out before me was unlike anything I'd ever experienced. My idea of fancy eating was going out for Chinese food when we went on vacation. This was a whole new level. I could barely believe it when I was served crocodile and all sorts of other melt-in-your-mouth delicacies. It was a menu extraordinaire. When we were all so full we couldn't bear to eat another bite, we shifted gears to the entertainment portion of the evening.

One of the parents who had been an actor and playwright before coming to the mission field had written a full-length musical theatre piece just for the occasion. The cast was composed of parents and teachers dressed up in the most ridiculous costumes, all handmade. The dialogue was laced with inside jokes for the students, and the night air was filled with boisterous laughter.

Sitting there in the audience I could barely believe my eyes when out onto the stage walked a group of mothers dressed in their daughters' clothes, most of them now sporting similar hairstyles, to perform a dance routine. This was not the disturbing part! When the last person paraded on stage, it was not my mother but my father! He was sporting a giant rack of fake boobs looking like they might burst out of the shirt he was stretching over top of my sister's sweat pants. For the entire routine those puppies bounced and jiggled while my father danced with shameless energy. The crowd went wild and people kept nudging me and whispering, as if I couldn't tell it was my father up there. I wanted to curl up and die.

But like all good things, the evening had to come to an end. The students gave a standing ovation as the cast, crew and cooks all took a final bow. We walked out of there knowing we were dearly loved. But the night of fun was not over. Oh no, it was just beginning.

A bunch of us pulled an all-nighter playing games, watching movies and reliving memories of our time together in PNG. We laughed and we cried and we dreamed. We promised we'd always stay in touch and we'd be friends for life. We took more pictures and drank more soda to keep ourselves awake. We wanted the day to go on forever.

I sat outside and watched the sun come up, painting the sky in brilliant pink and orange stripes. The clouds hanging just above the mountains turned from gray to violet to a rich purple. The chorus of nighttime insects sang their final tune, and then turned in for the day. I was going to miss this place and these people, even though they both drove me crazy from time to time. I was glad I hadn't skipped banquet, and grateful I hadn't run away because of all the drama. I stretched my legs and headed for home along the red dirt roads I knew so well. I looked at each house along the way. I knew every name of every person. I'd climbed almost every tree and run through nearly every yard. Every square inch had a memory. And then, with my eyes and legs feeling heavy, I rounded the hill and saw the little blue house on the corner where my bed awaited me. I was almost home.

This was the beginning of the end. After Banquet, graduation was not far behind. Once diplomas and awards were handed out and the valedictorian's speech had quickly been forgotten, it was time to go, time to fly away to distant worlds and start breaking all those promises about being friends forever and staying in touch. Time to put all those photographs into boxes to be quickly forgotten. It was time to keep living. But for one beautiful and glorious night of Banquet, none of the other stuff mattered. We forgot about the outside world and the new challenges awaiting us. We forgot about all the good-byes we would be saying in the days and weeks to come. We accepted the loving embrace of the community that had grown and nurtured us. We allowed ourselves one wondrous night, and made a few final memories.

The Wailing Wall

There are some things in life you can never understand until the moment arrives, no matter how well people to try to prepare you for them.

At the end of every school year in Ukarumpa we had Tissue Sunday when we said good-bye to the graduating seniors. The upstairs room where the high school students met for church was covered with rolls and rolls of toilet paper hanging from the rafters and wound around the chairs and benches, as if the whole room were being mummified and prepared for burial. Boxes of tissues were slowly circulated around the room throughout the service for those who used up all the neighboring TP they could get their hands on.

The service was designed to be a time of sharing. Up front on the stage stood an open mic beckoning to those brave souls who dared get out of their seats and face their peers with something to say. The beginning was always halting, with long pauses between people. Then slowly students began to realize that the time to say all of the things so long left unsaid was running out, and by the end there was a steady stream of students stepping up to say thank-yous and good-byes. Seniors with tear-filled eyes would give a few final words of advice, and brothers and sisters would weep as they said farewell to an older sibling. When our time was nearly up and the inevitable appalling sadness descended upon the room, the seniors were dismissed downstairs.

There awaited one final parting ritual. The seniors formed a long line downstairs along the far wall of the teen center basketball court, and all the middle schoolers and high schoolers made their way through the line giving hugs and handshakes. This emotional gauntlet became known as the Wailing Wall. As a middle schooler I did not fully understand what all the commotion was about, but every year as I got older and knew more and more people standing against the wall who were about to disappear from my life forever, it began to make more sense. Awkward handshakes with older kids I barely knew turned into long hugs and drawn out good-byes with teammates, fellow cast members and bandies. Each year the journey along the Wailing Wall took longer and hurt more. The emotional ache didn't stop at the door, but carried on like a dull background headache for days and even weeks. It was a painful reminder that this season wouldn't last forever.

And then suddenly it was me standing in the line along the Wailing Wall. I was the one crying like a baby, clinging to my childhood friends when the reality kicked in that this was it; there was no going back, there would be no last hoorahs. Somewhere between the awkward good-byes and the painful, gut-wrenching hugs with the people I cared for more than words could say, my heart broke. It happened at different points for all of us MKs, but the moment it hit you it was a crushing blow from which it took months and years to recover. To be honest, there is a part of me that is still recovering. There is a part of me still standing at the Wailing Wall.

You see, when we graduated from high school in Papua New Guinea we didn't get to hang around for the summer with our friends and then go to a college just an hour or two away. There was no staying at home to bum around while working part-time at the local pizza joint. Nope. When we graduated we hopped on a plane and flew away. Forever. I had many missionary friends who returned to PNG in later years hoping to find closure and peace, trying to rekindle and relive the beautiful moments of their past, only to find the Ukarumpa they knew was gone. It was but a memory of an age gone by. Yes, the houses and roads and even the trees were mostly the same, but the people they knew and loved had disappeared, leaving behind a strange new world vaguely resembling the one they remembered, but merely a pale, cruel imitation of their childhood.

When I sat strapped into my leather airplane seat the day after graduation I stared intently out the small round window when the plane began to accelerate down the runway. I looked at the tiny faces of friends and teachers and neighbors who had come out to the airstrip to say their last good-byes. I took a snapshot in my mind of their vigorously waving hands and their mouths formed into different shapes yelling only God knows what as their words were swallowed by the roar of the engines.

As the plane rose into the air and the people shrank into tiny black dots, I tried to catch one last glimpse of the large blue house on the corner I had called home and the dirt roads I had walked thousands of times as I grew from a child into a man. Through thick tears I watched it all fade away until nothing was left; my entire world was gone in the blink of an eye. The finality to that good-bye could not be undone. All that remained were my scars and stories of a childhood the world I was going to would never understand. For the first time in my life I was truly homeless and friendless, and it hurt so much I wanted to die.

Conclusion

It has been 14 years since I left PNG, and when I am asked where I'm from I still don't quite know how to answer. No matter what I say, there is a hesitancy. There is a sense that I'm not telling the truth because I exist between worlds. For so long I have battled against this reality. I have struggled with the ambiguity of my belonging, wanting to be from somewhere concrete, somewhere people know and understand, somewhere folks can find on the map.

I want to be able to give a simple answer to the simple question, "Where are you from?" But the reality is this: there is no simple answer. There is only one truth: I grew up between two worlds, and both worlds have shaped me into the man I am today.

I stumbled across this old poem that I wrote during my senior year of high school and the words of a struggling, pimple-faced youth still ring true today. They ring truer and deeper than I ever could have imagined, so I leave you with them.

Highlands Boy

Some say I'm strange, others just say nothing,

But all the while I can tell I don't belong.

Many think I'm crazy, but who are they to know?

They've never slept in round, dirt-floored bush huts,

Run deep through misty jungles in pounding rain,

Been bombarded by seas of swirling butterflies,

Or dived off soaring waterfalls into fresh crystal pools.

I've run down paths of hardened earth

And swum in oceans of deepest blue.

I've hunted wild boar, slimy crayfish and vibrant birds;

Watched tribal dances and slept beneath the starry heavens;

Lived a life of grand adventure in my little island world;

Seen the gruesome masks of war, powerful bows and cruel arrows;

Felt the warmth of an open fire toasting my bare, calloused feet;

And consumed native village foods like taro, sticky sago and boiled greens.

I've loved my fellow black brothers.

To me we are all the same;

Black or white makes no difference.

I am not from either world: the island or the new world.

There is nowhere for me to hide, for there is no place

For a kind of person with no home or race.

*Some would say I'm white, but I'm no more white than
black.*

They wonder why they cannot find where I belong.

The new world fails to look past my similar face

To the vast differences hidden beneath the surface.

Mysteriously, my life is sung to a different song.

I close my eyes and hear the pounding of wooden drums

Mingled with soft and comforting orchestral overtures.

The wild and frenzied dancing of the islanders

Fuses with the eclectic vibe of jazzy swing.

*The power of competing realms threatens to overwhelm
me;*

I feel the beat of two worlds deep within my bosom.

I am black and white and that is how I'll stay.

Made in the USA
Lexington, KY
29 July 2018